THE SPORT of MOTHERHOOD

Meredith,
Laugh a lot along the way...

Genevieve Butcher

THE SPORT of MOTHERHOOD

Training Tips for a Full & Balanced Life

Genevieve Hutcheson Butcher

Cover credit: Randy G. Marks

The Sport of Motherhood: Training Tips for a Full & Balanced Life
© Genevieve Hutcheson Butcher

First Edition, 2007

The Plain Paper Press

Mindzone, Inc.
All Rights Reserved

Printed in the United States of America

For information about permission to reproduce selections from this book, write to permissions, c/o Plain White Press LLC, 151 E Post Road, White Plains, NY 10601.

ISBN: 0-9760250-3-5
ISBN 13: 978-0-9760250-3-0

The Sport of Motherhood:
Training Tips for a Full and Balanced Life
Table of Contents and Chapter Summaries

Foreword by Demer Holleran vii

Acknowledgments viii

Introduction x

Chapter 1: Clarifying Your Objectives 1

How does a marathon runner do it? She matches her training to her objectives. Busy moms running the mom marathon can use the same road-tested techniques. I help you define and clarify your objectives, then introduce you to the "Whole Mom Food Groups" for optimum all-around health.

Chapter 2: Developing a Mom Strategic Plan 19

Once your goals and objectives are clear, you are ready to develop a plan of action. Follow my guidelines to create your own, customized strategic plan. I provide strategies for getting you started as well as some good advice about setting realistic goals, prioritizing goals, and finding the time you need.

Chapter 3: Teamwork at Home 31

Marathon runners look solitary in the race, but they benefit from the help and support of a well-organized team. For any mom, teamwork at home is critical. I help you lay a foundation for teamwork at home, where you need it most. We'll work on your philosophy of parenting, strategize about divvying up chores, and share some great tips for raising team players.

Chapter 4: Building a Personalized Support Network 54

Once you have a team at home, you can build a network of friends, family, and professionals who support you in your goals. That's what runners do to enhance their training and their races. I explain how to build a good network from scratch and how to personalize your network. I also point you to some existing support networks for moms.

Chapter 5: Mom Training Tips and Tools.. 80

You are ready for action, and this is the place. You have a plan and know how to set up a support network. Now I get you going. I help you to take those first steps, make more time for training, shed negative expectations, and keep track of your progress.

Chapter 6: Pacing and Endurance for Moms 103

Marathon runners have to pace themselves. Here I teach you pacing strategies to keep you progressing toward your goal. I discuss strategies for checking and adjusting your pace and show you ways to fuel up, recover, and keep going.

Chapter 7: Hitting Walls and Bouncing Back 123

Marathon runners call mile 18 "The Wall." It's when a runner's body is physically exhausted and her energy is gone. Moms hit the wall on a regular basis. Based on extensive interviews with moms, I identify the most common walls that moms hit and categorize them. I help you to examine your own personal patterns of hitting the wall and coach you on reading the signals, anticipating the wall, and training to get past it.

Chapter 8: Being Hit by a Truck 154

In this chapter, I address some of the toughest challenges that mothers face: accidents, deaths, miscarriage, raising a special needs child, divorce, and a long illness. These things change your life. I adapt the tools we discussed in Chapter 7 to help you see ways to cope with these events. You'll find pointers to experts, resources, and support groups here as well.

Chapter 9: Crossing the Finish Line and Getting the Goody Bag..173

It's time to celebrate those daily, weekly, and monthly personal victories. Most marathons give all participants a goody bag. My goody bag to you contains tips on everything from meals to managing multiples to travel.

Appendices 194

Research Questionnaire 213

Glossary 216

FOREWORD

I have known Genevieve since we were freshmen at Princeton University—twenty-plus years ago. She has never shied away from exploring new ways to tackle the everyday issues of life. Her idea here is new and a little startling. In typical Genevieve fashion, she has tested it thoroughly on family, friends, and research subjects. Her concept of motherhood as a marathon—a journey involving training, planning, and pacing—can help anyone take on and enjoy the new challenges of parenting.

To prepare to be your best competitively is a multifaceted problem. You need to balance many attributes: stamina, strength, speed, mental focus, and confidence. Being a grounded parent involves a similar balancing act. *The Sport of Motherhood* gives us the tools to fulfill our ultimate desire to become both great parents and accomplished individuals. At the same time, *Sport's* message is about being real, letting your hair down, identifying and addressing the obstacles that stop you, and not trying to do it all.

I am a longtime professional athlete and a recent new mother. The simple course outlined in *The Sport of Motherhood* has helped me rethink motherhood. I can approach motherhood with some overarching goals in mind just like I approach planning and implementing a successful training schedule. Then, as Gen says, I can strive to "pace for life while leading a full life." That means being realistic with where I am as a mother, an athlete, a businesswoman, a volunteer, and an individual. By identifying my priorities and knowing my limits, I can make everyday yes-and-no choices more easily.

Genevieve, the loving mother of four young children, has found a remarkable balance in raising them while conquering marathons, writing this book, and sharing her success through her TV show, parenting boot camps, support groups, and lectures around the country. We are fortunate that she has gone to the effort to share her tremendously helpful insights, and those gleaned from her many interviewees, with us all.

Well done, and thanks, Genevieve.

Demer Holleran
National Squash Champion, 1989–2004

ACKNOWLEDGMENTS

This book has been a labor of love. It has taken three years of interviewing, writing, and revising as well as laughter, sweat, and tears. It is a personal journey, as well as a discovery. It is difficult to let go because the words, the stories, and the experiences are still alive, inside me. But it is time, and I am ready to share it with you.

Thank you to the many wonderful people who so willingly opened up about their personal experiences so that others could benefit from their wisdom and not feel alone. You have truly made a difference!

My most heartfelt thanks go out to my husband, Keen, for helping me stay the course and pursue my dream. When I hit "walls" along the way, Keen reminded me that champions are made not by winning, but by being able to pick themselves up when they are knocked down, and persisting.

Thanks to my kids T. Keen, Lenox, Madeleine and Lilly for bringing laughter and joy into my days. Somehow, their presence always put things in perspective. I appreciate their input on my trademark name change to "Popillop Productions©," which is a unique rendition on Lilly's version of "Lollipop." We will find a way to use it!

I want to thank my mom and dad, Lenox Reed and Thad Hutcheson, and my brother Curtis Hutcheson for plowing through draft after draft of *Sport*, as well as my godfather Houghton Hutcheson for his support along the way.

I am grateful to my Butcher in-laws for their advice. My father-in-law, W. W. Keen Butcher, continues to shoot me hilarious emails in response to my *Sport* newsletters or updates. A special thanks to Alex French, Mandy Pagon, Leinie Brownell, Peggy Dunn, and Holly Pagon for their time, readings, and input.

I am grateful to some key mentors who assisted at various stages of the project: Daniella Russo, Susan Kraft, Carl Yorke, Gail Grant, and Jill Hargrave. Jill helped me stay in the day and enjoy the process, not worrying about the results. Daniella and Susan held my hand tight during the wild ride over the past year and a half and helped me walk through doors that opened along the way.

Thanks to my Dream Team: Suzanne Scott, Kathy Kroesche, and Joanie King. Not only have they assisted me as I map out my dreams, but also they have enabled me to figure out HOW to keep the balance and the pace manageable.

Thanks to my core group of cheerleaders and accountability buddies who read multiple drafts and gave input: Nancy Smith, Hazel Watson, Sarah Claytor, Jennifer Chernak, Laura Gilchrist, Nicole Laubscher, and Alison Byers.

I am also grateful to so many who have been incredibly supportive throughout this long journey with the book, especially: Stacey Archbell, Susan Phinney Silver, Cindy Campbell, Cheryl Tompkins, Valerie Sabbag, Alexis Sanford, Juana Aragon, Claudia Caballero, Rodney Aley, Ricardo Giancarlo Rico, Cindy Welker, Carol Hyde, and Dana Sands.

Thanks to my Publishing Team: Julie Trelstad and Christine Cervoni of the Plain Paper Press, designer Wendy Wolf, Daniella Russo and Mindzone Inc., and my terrific editor Veronica Kelly. What a trip this has been!

This book is in honor of some family members and a friend who passed away over the past few years: Genevieve McClendon, Jean Craver, Madeleine Kilvert Butcher, Bernie Butcher, and Jill Jacoby.

INTRODUCTION

I am not a supermom. I am just like many of you. Day in and day out, I have to balance the sometimes conflicting priorities of family, work, and personal pursuits. From my own experience with the challenges of motherhood and from interviews with over 300 women, men, and experts for this book, I realized that the sparkle of who we are can dim under the mother-loads of laundry, dishes, deadlines, financial stress, carpool schedules, and meal prep. I also realized that we can rekindle the spark and have a shot at our dreams during even the busiest stages of life. How? By honoring the pre-kid and post-kid part of ourselves even one hour a week, we can boost our spirits, minds, and souls. For some moms, this can mean making time to study a foreign language, photography or business skills; for others it can mean becoming a debate coach or real estate agent or writing a book. It can be about getting back into gardening, trying cycling or starting a realistic exercise routine. What it must mean is that you are honoring yourself.

I love my husband and four kids, and I also love running marathons, writing, painting, and creating and running *The Sport of Motherhood*. By applying marathon pacing strategies to other areas of my life, I am able to make room for some of my passions in the midst of raising young children. By clarifying my objectives, creating realistic timetables for manageable goals, prioritizing, and editing, I feel integrated and energized. I can put that zest back into my family, my marriage, my community, and my business.

This past year and a half has been unbelievably scary and rewarding. I feel like I have walked through fire on numerous occasions. I have reached outside of my comfort zone to learn how to: engage parent "experts" in speaker events and boot camps; produce and host a cable show; and launch and grow my business. Each time I got comfortable, I pushed again because I was ready to learn and try something else new and exciting. Sometimes I had a moment of clarity and wondered how the heck I thought I could do "this or that." So then I'd break "this or that" down into manageable chunks, stop analyzing, jump into the thick of it, and give it my best shot.

Had I gone back to teaching high school students or gone to work for someone else, I would have had a rollercoaster of a time, too. Just like other stay-at-home moms transitioning back to the workforce part time or full time, I had to get back into the swing of juggling family, school, carpool schedules, and volunteer and work commitments. I had to learn to fence work, streamline meal prep, and compartmentalize demands so that I could enjoy wherever I was right then, be it at a playground with the kids, on a date with my husband, at a boot camp with a group of moms, or on a cable show. My head needed to be in the game, in the moment, so that I could enjoy this ride.

For the past three years I have been applying *The Sport of Motherhood* tips and tools to my life and my business. The stories told by the women and men I interviewed float through my head and my days. If I am stuck or in a rut (for me that usually involves cooking or de-cluttering), I try out some strategies that worked for other moms and dads, even just to vary the pace a bit. When I hit walls, I have my support network and mentors in place who enable me to regain perspective and find my stride again.

My mantra has been: trust, believe, do. How do you know if you like something or are good at it until you try it? Rekindle or find a passion or interest and tap into it. See where it takes you. Populate your support networks (a dream team, entrepreneur group, or interest group) along the way to get ideas and feedback, and to gain confidence. Success is about trying, not about the end result. Who knows what opportunities will unfold?

I began this journey five years ago writing or drawing one hour a week. I had decided to make room for my passions, just a bit at a time. Two years ago, I sent this email to a few friends: "I have new wings, but I need to believe in order to fly."

Cheerleaders, accountability buddies, and mentors can walk with you to the doors of your life. Then you can take a deep breath, find the courage, and step through to see what is on the other side. What do you have to lose?

Try it. Do it. See what happens.

The Sport of Motherhood offers a wholesome training program for the challenges of life. Motherhood is not a competitive sport, but an endurance sport, much like marathon running. If we pool our resources and troubleshoot together, we can more fully enjoy the course of the day. *The Sport of Motherhood: Training Tips for a Full and Balanced Life* can help you pace yourself for life while leading a full life.

Supplies you'll need:

1. Notebook, journal, or computer file
2. Pen/pencil
3. Highlighters—at least 5 colors
4. Large wall calendar
5. Pack of index cards
6. Ruler

CHAPTER 1

Clarifying Your Objectives

> ▶ R U dog-tired of NOT keeping those healthy goals U set 4 yourself?
> ▶ R U ready 2 add a little zing 2 your bling?
> ▶ Or maybe you'd just like a bit of encouragement + practical advice?

It's all right here. So let's get going.

Welcome to *The Sport of Motherhood*, which is a little boot camp, a little TLC, a lot of game plan strategies, support, encouragement, and accountability. *The Sport of Motherhood* is a wholesome training program for the challenges of life. Motherhood is not a competitive sport but an endurance sport, much like marathon running. We mothers run a long race; we can learn some useful things from marathon runners and how they train. We need to understand ourselves and our distance. We need to learn to build our stamina and keep it over the long run. Then we can more fully enjoy each and every day as we move through the long years of our busy, beautiful marathon.

R U the person U want to B?

What gives you that spark? Do you want to kick-start a personal goal or new healthy habit? If you don't go for it, you may miss that experience completely. Waiting can become a habit for mothers. Wendy, a mom of three, sums this up nicely: "Women so often put things off (like careers or hobbies) until the next milestone. But there are always new milestones. After elementary school (a big milestone), there are new situations and needs. So they decide to put their plans off until after middle school. But [middle school] brings new challenges. Some women may never get to that career interest because they never get to the right milestone." For some mothers, the long-deferred goal is a second career. For others, it is a hobby, interest or talent that feeds the mind, spirit, and soul.

You don't have to wait until New Year's Eve to jumpstart a new endeavor. You can start now. You didn't miss the deadline. You also do not have to forsake family in order to make some time for your goal. Just one hour of personal goal-time a week can do the trick. How? That's where *The Sport of Motherhood* can help you build consistently to your goals.

Let's look at a runner training for a marathon. Her first task is to clarify her objectives so that her training matches her goals. For a first race, she might most want to make the distance and enjoy the race. For her next race, she might want to improve her time and run a strong finish. She'll train differently for each of these different races. Using *The Sport of Motherhood*, you too can clarify your objectives, set goals for yourself, and then make plans to reach them. You'll need to figure out what you want to do and how you are going to do it, taking into account where you are today. By having clear objectives, you can tailor your training to meet your goals and be ready to deal with the bumps and detours you meet during training.

Don't be surprised if your long-terms goals evolve or change as you go along your way. That is a good thing; it means you are open to new information and interests. Your journey is dynamic. It will change as you and your children grow and change. This chapter will help you get started by showing you how to establish your priorities and clarify your goals. You'll have both near-term goals for today and objectives for the future. Both are part of your training plan.

Figuring Out What You Need and Want: The Whole Mom Food Groups

Let's begin our sport of motherhood training together by first looking at what feeds the whole mom. Like anyone training for a long race, we moms need the right nutrition for both mind and body. To be whole and healthy moms, we need a balanced diet from different "food" groups. These groups express the different aspects of our lives. Just as our physical bodies need a balanced diet of proteins, fruits, vegetables, and grains, we need nourishment from different "whole mom" food groups to be healthy.

We need a bit of **SPICE**:

- **S**piritual Nurturance
- **P**hysical Nutrition and Exercise
- **I**ntellectual Stimulation
- **C**ommunal Sustenance
- **E**motional Comfort

Each of the SPICEs nourishes us in different ways, together making our whole person healthy and strong. Spiritual food gives us a better perspective on our lives and encourages us to think and feel more deeply. Physical food supplies the energy and stamina we need for our mental and physical activity. Intellectual food inspires us to be more interested and interesting. Communal food leads us to be compassionate and kind. Emotional food helps us to be warmer, gentler people. We moms are not the only ones to benefit from this good SPICE diet. When we eat right by feeding all aspects of our being, we win and our families win, too.

Spiritual Nurturance

We need to have food, or spiritual nurturance, to feed our souls. This includes nurturing our spirit, expressing ourselves, experiencing solitude, and making connections with the world beyond ourselves. This food creates space in the soul for an inner voice, nature, or God to speak to us.

What are your spiritual needs? Use a broad definition of "spiritual." Some moms can feed their souls simply by sitting quietly under a tree for a few moments and listening to the wind through the leaves. Others find strength in organized religion, a personal relationship with God, or a reverence for nature. In one *Sport of Motherhood* workshop, a mom exclaimed that laughter with other women fed some of her spiritual hunger. You may need solitude or meditation to connect with your core self. Do you know your spiritual needs? Do you address them?

For many moms, carving out time for some solitude is the key to recharging themselves. Others express themselves in dance or find a hobby that centers them. Everyone needs quiet time and some of us need more than others. Be honest with yourself about how much you need. Whether you write in a journal, read, sketch, or work on some poetry, the time you spend alone can energize you.

Emma, who has been a full-time, stay-at-home mom of two, recharges herself by finding time to be alone. She says, "Even an hour a week or half an hour a day, to let my thoughts still and my body relax, makes a difference. I think mommy brains have so many tracks going on—all at once all the time—that we need to just go to one track at a time for short periods, or else the signals get all tangled up and crossed!" Caroline, a full-time working mom of two, finds time for herself in the middle of the night. "Even if I am more tired then, at least I am reading some books and magazines so I feel more like a whole person. Exercise accomplishes this for a lot of women, but I find that the same time spent alone in a coffee shop writing in my journal or reading a book works for me—or just having the discipline to sit quietly."

For many moms, prayer time, a gratitude journal or meditation-through-yoga becomes a way to get grounded and feel restored and connected. Rubie, a stay-at-home mom of two, finds that "sleep, meditation, being physical, doing any sport restores me. Quiet time is when the kids are away from the house for awhile, at school, and after they go to bed." For Emma, spiritual time involves "figuring out what makes you feel spiritual and making time for it. It can be church, but for me it can also be writing in my journal, hiking or a meeting with a women's group."

A strong visual image can help you to strengthen your spiritual side. I view my week, and my life, as a path that I am building of gold bricks. I associate gold with purity and stability, safety, goodness and spiritual health, and I want these values to be the firm foundation beneath my feet. This vivid image—the gold brick path that I am building by hand—helps me select the best material to lay my path through each day. I don't want myself or my family to be hurt walking on rubble or rough and unstable ground. I know the gold bricks will support us, so I carefully place sound spiritual and meditative moments and activities in my week, such as: prayer/support groups, long meditative runs, church services, and a gratitude/prayer journal. I also carefully place spiritual or grounded people around my family because of their great value to me. I learn something from them just by being around their calm and their wisdom.

If I feel less connected at times, it is always because I have slacked on my spiritual and meditative work. By acknowledging my inattention, often to an accountability buddy, I can begin to reconnect. Within a week or two, at the most, I have regained my peace, my core, and my connection. I can see the gold brick path again. How do you replenish yourself?

Physical Nutrition

Physical nutrition includes healthy eating, exercise, and sleep. These are the things that keep your body going, healthy and strong. Part of taking care of yourself is addressing your physical needs.

Let's start with healthy eating. Do you already have an idea of where you could improve upon your eating patterns? Do you need to do more research because you feel stuck? How about consulting with a nutritionist who can help you tailor a plan to meet your individual needs and body type? I am not suggesting that you focus on diet, but on food as fuel. A car runs on gasoline. If it runs out of fuel, it stops. Moms are the same way.

So many women in the world are on diets trying to lose weight. The various fads and trends only serve to undermine a woman's health and well-being. These diets can produce rapid weight loss, but then the weight comes back. Even worse are the widespread eating disorders such as anorexia and bulimia. Unhealthy dieting and obsessing about food can be a real problem for moms. Moderation and pacing for the day and the week can bring about a change in attitude and well-being.

Carving out time for exercise may feel like an indulgence, but it is essential to your mental and physical well-being that you find some time to move and work your body. When you take care of yourself, those who depend on you benefit. You feel better, have more energy and are able to give more freely and easily. Gloria, a career mom of three kids, talked about how she couldn't seem to take time for herself and so became bitter and resentful. As she noted, moms just "give, give, give. For years I didn't take care of myself and did everything for everybody else. What did that get me? A load of resentments. Finally, I woke up . . . **if the mother is not happy, everything falls apart**."

Now Gloria makes time to work out. As a result, she feels happy in herself and good with her family. "Let's face it. When you work out, you feel better about yourself. I don't ever want to go back to that place [of resentments] again." Her family noticed the change, too and benefits from it.

> ## Mom Tip
>
> "I woke up this morning and everyone wanted to do something different. My son wanted a haircut. My daughter wanted to go to the bank . . . I made breakfast for everyone and then went right [to my workout]. I need to take care of myself. Then I can go home ready to do all those things. Working out makes me stronger, a better lover, and happier in the home—ready to tackle laundry, dishes, everyday chores, and meet others' needs." —Gloria

Caroline, another full-time working mom, says, "For a long time I wanted to spend every spare minute when I wasn't working with the kids—except for my Saturday date nights with my husband. That resulted in slow, steady weight gain. Now I know I've got to exercise a few days a week." Caroline's regular exercise helps her to feel better about herself and improve her health and state of mind.

If you are in shape, you can more easily keep up with your kids. Running and playing are part of an active motherhood. Motherhood is physically demanding, with all of the lifting and carrying of children, toys, laundry, groceries, and diaper bags. Strong abdominal muscles can help prevent back injury. Though I contend with a bad back, I know that I am far less likely to injure it when I use my leg and abdominal muscles to lift properly. Exercise keeps me fit and sound and teaches me how to use my body well. As the kids get older, I can rollerblade, bike, run, play soccer, basketball, and hockey with them.

> **Mom Story**
>
> You can also vary your exercise and partner up with a spouse. Suzanne says, "It is important that hobbies change." She took up golf a couple of years ago because she "could stay healthy and active. Golf was also something I could do with my husband, and it got me out. So it fit into my strategic plan."

Build exercise into your days. Walk whenever possible, whether you are doing your daily errands or picking up your kids at school. Take the stairs instead of an elevator if the distance is reasonable. Pick a family sport that you can all enjoy, such as skiing, tennis, hiking, cycling, or swimming. Shoot some hoops outside with the kids to get your blood pumping. You can jog while your child scooters or rollerblades. Thanks to baby joggers, even moms with infants and toddlers can combine exercise and mothering.

All of the moms I interviewed were aware of how much sleep they needed and how they usually fell short. You may never be able to get all the sleep you want while your kids are still at home, but you need to get enough to function well. Do you know how much you need? People's sleep needs vary. Some need more and some less. How much do you actually get?

Try this to estimate how much sleep you need: Go to bed earlier than usual for a week and log in the hours you sleep. When your body has the opportunity to take more sleep, does it? Did you end up sleeping until your usual wake-up time, thus getting more sleep? Or maybe you found yourself getting up earlier than usual because you'd had enough sleep. Average the time that you slept during the last four nights of that week. By that time, your body will have adapted to the new bedtime schedule, enabling you to fall asleep earlier more easily. Use that average as your Sleep Ideal—it should be just about the amount of time you need to spend sleeping in order to get a good night's rest.

Many moms trade sleep for personal time. Arlene is currently a stay-at-home mom of three. For her, "the evenings after the kids are down are my time to read. Sometimes I read until 2:00 a.m. and am tired the next day. But I love it. I love my reading time at night. I read lots of books." The following night she goes to bed earlier to balance things out.

Other moms make sleep more of a priority. Melanie, who works part time and is a mom of two, says, "I need my eight hours and get it." Otherwise she is "not a happy camper." Pat, a full-time working mother, meets her sleep needs. "I actually get a decent amount of sleep—generally eight hours, sometimes less. I don't know that I have felt really rested for quite some time. Perhaps following a vacation, but with children . . . you never seem to get lots of extra rest."

Yet another mom, Elizabeth, acknowledges the price she pays for her lack of sleep: "I find that if I don't get a good night's sleep, I have a much lower tolerance for cranky kids and a much harder time getting through the day." By keeping your specific sleep needs in mind, you can more fully enjoy the pace of the day or the week.

Intellectual Stimulation

Intellectual stimulation exercises your brain. You need intellectual food to keep you sharp, interested, and growing. Reading can take you to other cultures, teach you how to do something new and connect you with the past. Curiosity is intellectual hunger. The more you know, the more you can be an informed mom and the better you can teach your children.

The big joke about motherhood is that once you have a baby, you go brain dead or can't string a sentence together. Okay, I agree in part, but there are special circumstances. New babies and sleep deprivation can temporarily take away mental sharpness. Toddlers turn on all of your danger radars, and it requires a lot energy and focus to run those radars. Which electrical outlet, Band-Aid, bug, paper clip, pebble or small toy will your child try to eat today? Then you have the curious runners who want to dart away from you in the parking lot, at the store or at a playground. Finally, you have to negotiate the daily "No!" and "I can do by self!" dramas that sap your energy. And what about all those sleepless nights due to musical beds, teething, illnesses, or a thousand other small interruptions?

No wonder I could not pick up any serious literature for the first few years after having kids! Instead, I collapsed into bed exhausted and could only read a few pages of lighter fare such as mysteries and thrillers before falling asleep. Of course I also read parenting manuals, but in my mind at the time that didn't even seem to count as reading. I remember trying to re-read some William Faulkner and James Joyce novels and giving up. "Later," I thought. I was sure that someday I would get my mind back. Well, someday came, and I did get it back.

What kind of intellectual food do you need or crave? Do you feel a bit lost or empty at times? Whether you are working or staying at home, you can add books on tape or music to your walks and car rides. Multitask and enjoy the journey. Some moms I interviewed found that book club deadlines pushed them to read more books and add more variety to their book diet. The ensuing discussions "were stimulating." Others sought noncredit or credit classes related to personal goals or career training.

Still others traded a little sleep time for personal time. Several moms work late into the night to make time for an intellectual passion. Barbara, a mom of two who works part time, says, "I am a night owl and love to stay awake in the wee hours of the morning. I do great artwork when my brain is clear and the silence is unmistakable."

Katia talks about her relatively new passion for photography, which has begun to supply part of her intellectual stimulation. When her youngest was in kindergarten, she was ready to pursue some of her own interests. "If I didn't do my own thing, I would overwhelm the kids. I would drive them nuts giving them idea after idea, living through them." Katia began taking a photography class and became hooked. "When I go and start clicking and clicking, I can't rest until I see what comes. . . ." Stimulated and committed, she worked her photography in around the family schedule. Several years later, she has both solo exhibits and is part of group exhibitions. "I haven't felt so well in years. I am happy. Not making much money, but fulfilled."

Many moms who pursue professional work count on the additional income but they also note other benefits, such as the intellectual satisfaction and autonomy that their profession gives them. Su, a part-time working mom of two, seeks "mental stimulation—I work for organizations that I feel strongly about—reproductive health, domestic violence, etc. I love the issues, and so enjoy the work. Second, working part time keeps me in the loop. At some point, I will go back to work full time."

Teresa, a research scientist who is a mom of two, says, "I work because I love what I do and I am good at it!" Finally, Chaille, a marriage and family therapist who works part time and has two children, writes, "I work because I love it, I need the income and because I find that working away from them makes me enjoy coming home and being with them. The balance works for me most of the time."

Communal Sustenance

With your children, you have a built-in community, but you need adult interaction as well. Your husband or partner is a key part of your adult community but cannot meet all of your social needs. Communal sustenance involves building friendships and relationships with a wider circle of those in our lives, including our extended family (in-laws, uncles, aunts, and cousins), our old and new friends and our neighbors.

Emma puts the modern mom's role in a historical context. A "key theme is not being an island. The main reason that so many of us are overstressed is the advent/predominance over the past 50 to 100 years of the 'nuclear family.' Mothers used to have much more balance when there were grandmas, etc., in the house to help out (and the grandmas had more balance, too!). Not that the old days were idyllic; moms were out working in the fields, etc., but I do think that the system of isolated nuclear families needs to be supplemented by finding support systems locally."

Some moms seek the connection, accountability, and camaraderie found in groups and classes such as book clubs, prayer groups, photography lessons, dance and yoga sessions, writing seminars, or continuing education classes. Others draw on the support offered in mothering circles. Play groups, mothers' groups, and school hubs are great places to find kindred spirits. Other moms turn to their tried-and-true friendships for a good dose of lively conversation.

Linda, who has been both a full-time working mom and a stay-at-home mom of three, finds her connection in three main places: a prayer group, the moms at the YMCA, and "four very special friends whom I can tell anything and not be judged."

Dana, a stay-at-home mom of two, built her support structure by "cultivating friends—seeking friends who do not have family nearby, getting involved at church, school, and the Junior League which helps to make friends, recruiting and retaining low-cost babysitters." When Dana addresses the issue of balance, she says, "the single most critical thing for me is to find time with other adults. Either for bonding (friends) or for sense of accomplishment (volunteer work)."

Stella, a full-time working mom of two, finds her communal food another way. She likes tennis and jogging, but does not have much time for them. She says there are "many sacrifices" right now at this stage of raising young children. Every few weeks, her husband will take the kids and she meets with a girlfriend for coffee or lunch to talk. "We can really talk without the children." If time allows, they may even get to go shopping together afterwards. "I go back home and feel good, recharged." This friendship connection charges her for a while until it is time for the next friendship outing.

How do you connect with others? Write down all the ways that you build community for yourself. What works for you? These notes will help you with Chapter 4, which is about assessing friendships and building support networks.

Emotional Comfort

Is there a mom who hasn't set her emotions aside over and over again in order to take care of someone or something? Moms nurture others, but our emotions need our attention, too. We need to feed them and express them in appropriate ways. Some of us fight our emotions; we sometimes view them as weeds, intruders in our beautiful garden. We try to suppress them and live by logic, but they are part of our lives. We need to learn to recognize them, acknowledge their existence, and then deal with them if they are difficult or enjoy them if they are positive.

> **MOM TIP**
>
> Have you noticed that smiles are contagious? Did you know that it takes more muscles to frown than to smile? How you interact with the world each day affects other people. If you are grumpy and bitter, you can sap energy from those around you. Those who have clear boundaries will probably give you some space. Others, including your children, might realize that it really is a "terrible horrible very bad day" (Judith Viorst's *Alexander and the Terrible, Horrible, No Good, Very Bad Day*) and go on to frown at someone else. I am not saying that you need to fake a smile, but can you do something about what is bugging you?

It seems like a lot of moms have a run-in with resentments when it comes to how they parent or raise their children. Your children learn from you. If you are basically a resentful person, they can become resentful as well. If you are happy, they can learn to look at the positive side of things. If you shut your emotions in, they might, too.

How do you handle resentments? What do your resentments typically involve? Is the source conflicting parenting styles, different goals, unclear boundaries, too many responsibilities, societal or familial expectations? Something else? Roberta, a mom of two who works part time from home, says, "Resentments for me come in the form of me feeling like I don't get the same amount of free time that my husband does on the weekends—that the babysitting duties are all lopsided. It comes from not feeling appreciated or acknowledged for all the hard work I do 'just as a mom.' I also get resentful when family does something against my wishes or differently than I would with my kids. It's clear I need some balance...."

Clear the air. Just try new ways until you figure out what works for you. Thumb through some self-help books on your topic of need or interest. Get professional help if you need it. Karina has learned this: "I am very open in communication and can't hold much in with my own family. I've had to learn to be more diplomatic at home and wait until I'm not emotional to share my resentments. With others, I try to be straightforward, nonpersonal, issues-based but also to not hold things in unless there's really nothing to be gained from it."

> **Mom Story**
>
> Kathleen says that she and her husband work daily on clear communication. "We are huge 'scorekeepers' and are trying to unlearn this behavior. My mother-in-law, while well meaning, is an expectational nightmare, a righteous boundary smasher, who is unwilling to cut the umbilical cord from the son she has trained to see her as a martyr. (Do I sound bitter?) Some books have helped me a ton—Dale Carnegie's *How to Win Friends and Influence People* and Sarah Napthali's *Buddhism for Mothers*. I try to put things into perspective, to humble myself and to view these resentments as challenges to better improve my people-management skills and my patience."

Chaille says that she is "learning to talk about [resentments] with a person, if I feel I need to or want to save the relationship, or I let them go by talking to my husband and praying to let go."

Get rid of the baggage. Lighten your mood. Find and keep the joy. (More ideas on how to lighten your load are in Chapters 6 and 7.)

Develop Your SPICE List

Now it is time to fill in your **SPICE** list. You will use this SPICE list to develop your Strategic Plan in the next chapter, so take some time to think about your answers. Remember, nurture yourself and you will be better equipped to nurture your children.

1. Write your current interests, activities, and goals in each of the SPICE categories.
2. Now add interests and activities that you would like to pursue if you actually had the time, with goals for each.

Please note that some categories overlap. That is fine. Just try to put a few items in each category.

S _____
P _____
I _____
C _____
E _____

If you want to flesh out your SPICE list a bit more but are not sure how, give the exercises at the end of this chapter a try. These exercises can help you identify some long-term interests and goals and preview your *Sport of Motherhood* course. Not all of the exercises speak to every mother, so feel free to choose the ones that might work for you. You might want to consider starting up a notebook or special file in your computer for your answers.

We are both mothers and individuals. It is easy to lose touch with what makes us tick as we meet the needs of family, work, and other responsibilities. Many moms tell me that there are just not enough hours in the day. By carving out and protecting one hour a week for personal interests, a mom can recharge and honor that pre-kid or post-kid part of her. An hour a week is manageable. I believe that we need to keep growing alongside our kids and keep the SPICE in our lives.

With your SPICE list in hand, you now have all the elements that you need to create your training plan: your SPICE needs and the goals you want to work towards. In the next chapter, we'll look at how to fit these into your life.

EXERCISES

Warm Up: Reflective Stretches

Imagine Your Future Self

Imagine what you will be like forty years from now. Find words to describe the kind of person you would like to be in your later years. Mentally try on a lot of personal styles to see what future self appeals to you.

You might be adventurous, spirited, carefree, a queen bee, kind, happy, ambitious, involved in global or community concerns, athletic, artistic, active, an educator, prolific, free-spirited, vengeful, bitter, depressed, family-oriented, successful in career choices, healthy, sober, spiritual. . . . The possibilities are almost endless, but with some focus you can imagine a future self that you like and admire. How does this exercise help you to organize your objectives? It gives you the long, long view on your life, and that can relieve some of the pressure and near-sightedness of the present.

After you have imagined a future self, take out your *Sport of Motherhood* journal or a notebook. Free-write for five to ten minutes on the following questions:

- How would you like to be remembered in forty years, and what values, accomplishments, people, and places would be important to you?
- If you could live the next forty years doing whatever you wanted, how would you spend that time?
- List the things you would like to be involved in over the next forty years (family, career, politics, marathons, triathlons, yoga, dance, squash, tennis, art, writing, teaching, cooking, gardening, music, concerts, outreach, education, church, community, grandmothering, etc.).
- Write down where you would like to be living (in a particular city, on a farm, in the mountains, on an island, in another state, in a less expensive area or all over as world traveler).
- With whom?

- List ten words that you would like to describe your life. Choose from the following list or use your own words.

    Accomplished, active, adaptable, adventurous, agile, alive, ambitious, analytical, animated, appreciative, articulate, athletic, aware, balanced, beautiful, beloved, benevolent, bold, brave, calm, candid, carefree, careful, cautious, challenged, cheerful, clean, clever, comfortable, committed, compassionate, compatible, confident, connected, content, courageous, crafty, creative, curious, delighted, determined, diligent, disciplined, driven, dutiful, easygoing, effervescent, empathetic, energetic, enlightened, enthusiastic, excellent, excited, faithful, family-oriented, fearless, flexible, focused, forgiven, forgiving, free, friendly, fruitful, funny, generous, gifted, giving, good listener, good parent, graceful, gracious, grateful, grounded, happy, healthful, healthy, honest, honorable, hopeful, humble, illuminating, imaginative, independent, inquisitive, insightful, inspired, intellectual, intense, introspective, involved, joyous, kind, leader, liberated, light, literary, literate, loving, loyal, mature, meditative, meek, merciful, mindful, missionary, motherly, multitasking, musical, nice, nurturing, open-minded, optimistic, organized, orgasmic, passionate, patient, peaceful, peace-loving, pensive, perceptive, persistent, philanthropic, playful, positive, pure, reflective, rejuvenated, relaxed, reliable, religious, respectful, responsible, scientific, selfless, self-reliant, self-sufficient, skilled, soaring, sober, smart, spirited, spiritual, steady, strong, succinct, talented, team player, tenacious, thorough, thoughtful, thrifty, trusting, trustworthy, unburdened, unwavering, upbeat, virtuous, whimsical, willing, wise, witty, worldly, young, youthful

- Now circle the words that surprise you or that you would like to focus on given the time and the means to do so.

- List five to ten things that you would like to have accomplished by the end of your life.

Practice: New Skills

Define Your Values

List five values (or virtues) that are important to you. I make some suggestions below to get you started. They are adapted from *Marguerite Kelly's Family Almanac: A Helpful Guide to Navigating Through the Everyday Issues of Modern Life* by Marguerite Kelly and Katy Kelly and "31 Ways to Pray for Your Children" by Bob Hostetler.

> Attention to Others, Balance, Charity, Compassion, Consideration, Contentment, Courage, Courtesy, Curiosity, Enthusiasm for Life/Learning, Fairness, Faith, Fortitude, Generosity, Graciousness, Gratitude, Growth in Grace, Heart for Missions, Honesty and Integrity, Hope, Humility, Joy, Justice, Kindness, Love, Loyalty, Mercy, Modesty, Openness, Peacemaker, Perseverance, Prayerfulness, Prudence, Purity, Respect (for self, others, authority), Responsibility, Salvation, Self-Control, Self-Discipline, Thoughtfulness, Tolerance, Willingness and Ability to Work

Once you have your list, think of at least five things that you can do TODAY to support those values and virtues in your life.

Listen to Those Escape Fantasies

Do you ever have escape fantasies, even for a moment? Where does your head go when you are doing all those mundane, routine tasks, like washing dishes, folding laundry or commuting to work? Are you thinking about travel, time alone, dancing, reading? Is there a familiar pre-mom or a future interest floating around in your daydreams?

These escape fantasies can be very revealing and perhaps become a new fulfilling goal. You just might be able to incorporate one of these dreams into your life right now. In my workshops, some moms long for a few carefree travel days, time to play a musical instrument again or to continue their education. Still others just want to go out dancing every once in awhile. Believe it or not, you can bring your longing into your current phase of motherhood with a bit of purpose. Jot your ideas down so that you have them to refer to when you are feeling less grounded. They can help you refocus.

Recognize Your Guiding Passions

What are you passionate about? If your answer is "my children" and "my partner," that's great. What else are you passionate about? Don't worry about whether you are good at it or not; just list a few things that motivate you, capture your interest, or make work feel like play. This is an important list to return to if you feel lackluster and unmotivated.

Speaking of Play

How do you play? When, where or with whom do you feel playful? List five things that encourage you to feel playful, get giddy, be like a kid (it can be a playground, a movie, ice cream, a theme park, or zoo time with the kids; it can be reading the newspaper comics; it can be making sand castles, swimming in the big waves, or collecting shells at the beach; seeing chick flicks, playing with puppies, flying a kite, sailing with your partner, enjoying a date night, exploring new restaurants and cities with your partner or a friend; it can be family driving trips and vacation times).

Cool Down

Rediscover Your Hobbies and Interests

List your hobbies and interests. Now list five new ones that you would like to explore sometime soon. If your mind is blank, maybe you just need to make time to think so that meaningful ideas can bubble up. Your first hobby can be about making and protecting downtime! Update this list periodically to see which things emerge as long-term interests.

A Thought about Hydration

I think that each mother needs two water bottles: one for parenting and one for herself. Raising kids is both wonderful and challenging. It is also life-giving and exhausting. The parenting water bottle might be one-on-one time with the kids or good old-fashioned family fun, be it playing board games, taking a trip to the beach, or having dinner together. Moms also need to rehydrate themselves, and a personal water bottle will mean something different to each mom. My personal water bottle involves time with my husband, a weekly long run in nature, a good laugh with a friend, and something that taps my passion, which would be the creative aspects of putting together and running *The Sport of Motherhood.*

CHAPTER 2

Developing a Mom Strategic Plan

> ▶ R U sprinting through your weeks?
> ▶ Can U identify the obstacles that R stopping U from being who U want 2 B?
> ▶ Do U want 2 make the time 4 something that will help U feel more grounded N your daily life?

Great work in Chapter 1! Now you have your SPICE list—a short list of goals that are important to you. If you have arrived here with a single goal, that's great, too. You're focused and ready to train. Next you will create a strategy for reaching your objectives. Moms are bombarded by distractions. This chapter will help you develop a strong, mom-specific strategic plan to keep you on course. Your strategic plan will establish priorities and define boundaries within your objectives. Without a good plan, you are running in the dark.

What Is a Strategic Plan?

In the last chapter, you created the list of the things you want in your life. Your next decision is how to incorporate these things into your current life. You'll probably have to reorganize your days. Old habits and routines may have to go. You have new, clear goals to accommodate. Ask yourself what you must change to advance from what you did today to what you will do tomorrow. These are important decisions that only you can make. A simple strategic plan can be your vehicle for change.

Your plan will provide a framework for you to make decisions easily as they come up. First, and very importantly, it will help you judge if a new opportunity will further your goals. Mothers' lives can be full to overflowing with opportunities for new activities and interests. If you accept too many of them, you can end up going in too many directions at once, feeling scattered and drained. You'll use your strategic plan to evaluate all those opportunities quickly and fairly. Second, your plan will help you assess whether or not an opportunity is a good one. Not every relevant opportunity is a good one *for you*. Your strategic plan helps you decide *will this work for me?* Will it increase or drain my energy? Will it encourage or discourage me? Will it move me forward?

> **MOM TIP**
>
> Stick to your plan or change your plan. It is there to help you. If it is cast in stone, it is likely to sink like a stone. If your situation changes, be flexible enough to adapt to the new situation.

By channeling your efforts through your plan, you will be energized, focused, and able to move forward. By keeping a strategic plan in mind, you free yourself up to say yes to yourself and no to others. Does this sound selfish? Not once you think about it. You don't do anyone any good if you spread yourself too thin. Why not be more selective with how you use your time?

So what does a strategic plan contain? Simply put, it is a road map to your goals. It lays out where you want to go, the steps you'll take to get there, the potential obstacles you'll meet, and how you will overcome them. It articulates both what you want to accomplish and how you can do it. It's your training plan.

A Word about Goals

Before you start your plan, you need to do a sanity check on your list of goals and make sure they are *manageable* and *realistic*. What does manageable mean to you? Maybe unmanageable is easier to define.

Do you ever feel a knot in your stomach or feel your body tense up when you think of your upcoming schedule or responsibilities? If so, you are anxious about something. Maybe you're experiencing a moment of reasonable anxiety—for example, if you're about to put yourself on the line about something, present an idea or paper to a group, hold an event or make a speech. If not, your anxiety could relate to the kind of commitment or level of commitment you are making. Are you stretching yourself in a positive way or does your schedule make you feel short-tempered with others? Maybe you need to cut back and set more manageable or realistic goals. You have a whole life to live. You don't have to cram everything into the present week.

> **Mom Story**
>
> Karina uses both writing and reflection to help her be more realistic about her goals. "I put down critical steps toward reaching the goal on paper. Then I add a timeline. Then I pray that God help me by opening or closing doors to lead me where He wants me to go. Then I sit in the grey. As a black-and-white person, I have a hard time waiting, deciding, and not moving. I've learned to rest in the grey and take it as a peaceful time and trust that I will be led in the right direction in time—just not my own time frame. Most of all, as a mom I don't set high goals! My goals are very basic—exercising three times a week, cooking healthy dinners for my family, and making quiet time with my Bible." Moderation brings about a steady pace for the day, for the week, for one's life.
>
> Chris uses pen and paper to physically edit her list and gain perspective. "Goals and objectives that seem unattainable tend to stress me at first, and then after a good night's sleep and hot shower, I make a list of all the things that need to happen to reach the goal and then prioritize it. What things can be combined and what things aren't really necessary. I get a sense of pleasure crossing things off a physical list."

Take into account where you are today and go from there. Margaret notes: "My biggest problem is that I'm not realistic about how much time things take . . . and then [I] get down because I just don't get much accomplished." Create your own realistic finish lines and short-term intermediate mile markers given your unique daily and weekly family and work schedules.

> **MOM TIP**
>
> If you shoot for the sky with your goal, you will shoot yourself in the foot. Sure, you can meet an unrealistic stretch goal for a few weeks or maybe a month, but you cannot run on adrenaline for weeks on end. One week you won't be up for it; instead of even trying to do part of the goal, you give up and don't do any. The next week it will be easy to do the same. Then you get down, and feel like a failure.
>
> Feeling like a failure only saps your energy and enthusiasm, making it even harder to begin again. If you establish a more realistic baseline, you will be able to better pace yourself and succeed. Each week's success brings more energy and, in turn, fuels and inspires you for the next week.

I like to keep a goal calendar. It's a great place to log progress and jot down ideas. If you do not have a goal calendar, you might want to make one by purchasing or creating a new calendar. You can also add your goal time to your usual calendar using a different color pen or highlighter. The different color helps you to see time invested in your goal at a glance. You can quickly find your time over the week and total it.

Be sure to log your thinking time on a goal calendar. Thinking counts as research towards your goal. When you see your goal planning written down, it helps you to keep your expectations concrete and realistic.

Note the goal total for each week on every Sunday or Monday, depending on your calendar and your preference. I designate Mondays as GOAL TOTAL days because weekdays have more room on my month-by-month Microsoft Outlook© calendar than weekends. Even if you don't use a calendar, make note somewhere of the time you spend on your goal.

Now that you have picked a realistic, priority goal (or two), it is time to ask yourself, "How can I prepare myself to reach my goal? What steps will I take?" Now it is time to create a Strategic Plan.

How to Develop a Strategic Plan

First, take out your SPICE list from Chapter 1. It includes your notes of all the things you want to add to your life. One of the important things to remember is that what you want most may be the hardest thing to do. Some things also take more time than others. Still others may not take much time at all and yield great benefits.

Use a scale from 1 to 10 to rank your goals, with one being the top priority. Some goals may share the same ranking. For our example, we'll use an imaginary mother, Alexis. She is a stay-at-home mother with two boys, three and five, and a husband in high tech. She has these things on her **SPICE** list and has written her **priority rankings** next to each item:

> **S**piritual: get out in nature (hiking? gardening? going to the park?) 2, meditate more (classes?) 5
> **P**hysical: more sleep 4, exercise regularly 4, vary kind of exercise when in a rut (hiking, jogging, tennis, yoga, aerobics) 6
> **I**ntellectual: read good books 3, learn some new computer skills 4
> **C**ommunal: connect with some other people 3, expand circle of friends and include some accountability buddies and mentors 3, talk about interesting things 3
> **E**motional: let my husband know regularly how much I love him 1; date night 2
> Other goals: learn Tae Kwon Do or kickboxing 10, learn to knit 9

First, look at any ones and twos in your list since they are marked with the highest priority. For Alexis, it jumped out at her that she needed to express her love to her husband more often, set up date night, and get out in nature more, in that order. Next, she'll try to read some good books, expand her circle of friends, talk about interesting things. Finally, she'll move on to the lower-priority items like exercising more and learning to knit.

> ## Mom Tip
> You want to <u>start</u> only one thing at a time, but once you have that one going, you can add others onto your plate, one at a time.

The next thing you want to look for is what I call *double-and-triple* duty items. Are there some activities that combine different goals, like getting more exercise by hiking in nature? Examine your list for double-duty activities. Alexis looked at her list and saw both (1) reading and (2) connecting with people and talking about interesting things. Then she remembered that there was a book group she had been thinking about joining. The book group would help her to read some good books, introduce her to some new people and the conversation would be interesting! That's what I call *power-goaling*!!

Prioritizing goals can help you, but listen to your heart as well. Alexis really wanted to connect better with her husband, so she decided to start with that first. Sometimes a high-priority goal will jump out at you like that, but not always. Use an overview plan to give yourself a new perspective on your goals. The easiest way to create your overview plan is to set up a simple table. It's amazing how putting your goals into a table helps you see how they relate to each other, the kind of effort each one requires, and what benefits each will bring you. Here's Alexis's Overview Strategic Plan:

Alexis's Overview Strategic Plan Table

PRIORITY	Goal	Getting There	Current Status	Obstacles	Resources	Allies	Next Step	Payoff
1	Improve relationship with Will	Let Will know how much I love him via cards, emails, focus time	Awareness of the problem, ideas for change	Exhaustion, time, reciprocation	Friends, babysitter	Family	Cards	Strengthen marriage
2	Get some exercise while getting recharged spiritually and mentally	Go hiking regularly in local parks with Susan	Desire	Time, guilt	ABC Park, BC Lake	Susan, Will	Find time on calendar, write "Nature Date"	Grounded, centered, energized
3	More adult intellectual connection	Join the book club	Desire	Time, guilt	Babysitter	Will	Get details	More fulfilled, happier

Notice how Alexis uses the table to organize her training so that she isn't overwhelmed by details. She takes the very specific ideas in her SPICE list (let my husband know I love him, date night) and makes them into a high-level goal: "Improve relationship with Will."

Filling Out Your Overview Strategic Plan Table

Now it is your turn. Set up your own **Strategic Plan Table** using Alexis' overview table as a model. Like Alexis, put the highest priority items at the top of your table, always keeping in mind that you can change their order anytime. Notice the categories in the table headings. These help Alexis transform her goal from a dream into a truly workable plan with simple and familiar component parts. She can do this!

Here is a quick run-down of each category. Your **Goal** is what you want to achieve, your objective. For Alexis, this is improving her relationship with her husband. **Getting There** is a summary of how you plan to reach your goal. With a high-level goal like Alexis', the items in **Getting There** are often smaller, intermediate goals. **Status** expresses where you are today with that goal. **Obstacles** are things that could prevent you from reaching your goal. Notice that the overview table requires just brief notations in the **Getting There**, **Status**, and **Obstacles** categories. When an item definitely reaches the top of your list, and you are ready to implement your plan, you'll approach **Getting There**, **Status**, and **Obstacles** in much more detail.

The overview table can really reveal connections among your priorities. In one *Sport of Motherhood* Workshop, a mom of three talked about sleep deprivation as an obstacle to her goals. Her overview table helped her see that before she could work on exercising more, eating healthier foods, or finding a hobby, she needed to take care of basic sleep needs. Her strategic plan involved teamwork at home to get past this obstacle and help her get a good night's sleep at least every other night.

Resources are things and activities that help you overcome the obstacles. You can go to the library to research an issue, talk to a nutritionist, or consult handbooks on time management. These are all resources.

Allies are the people who can and will help you. Be honest and realistic with this category. Who can truly support you and encourage you in your endeavors? Don't forget to assess your immediate and extended family, your friends and neighbors.

Because we live in a culture of self-reliance, many moms struggle with asking for help. Be realistic about who can help you, but don't be too shy when it's time to ask. If you reach out, you also bring others into your life. It makes people feel good and more connected to help someone out. You can do the same for someone else another time. (If you want to expand your allies and support network, leave some blank space in your table and come back to this category after you have read "Chapter 4: Building a Personalized Support Network.")

What is your **Next Step**? Think of at least one specific thing you can do today that will move you towards your goal. Keep it practical. Your next step could be as simple as buying a card, getting one or two supplies, or making a dinner list. If you are absolutely not sure about your Next Step, then put down something like "gather details" or "get more information" and then commit to doing some research.

Finally, **Payoff** explains why achieving this goal is important to you. What is the main benefit it brings to you?

After you have gone over Alexis' sample table and you are comfortable with all the categories, give your own table a try. You do not need to flesh out the details for all of your objectives. Instead, prioritize them and focus on a few. When you are ready to add some new objectives, then create categories for those. At this stage, it's better to work with a few main goals.

Use the table below, or make a copy of it in your notebook or computer file (an Excel or Word table works well). Take your SPICE list priorities and use them to fill in the first one or two rows. High-level goals, like improving a family relationship, are often very important. You can also add short-term, daily goals such as reading more, keeping on top of clutter, or adding variety to dinner meals. You can stop with one or two goals, or you can fill the chart out completely and then decide later which goals to focus on. If you would like to see another example of a Strategic Plan Table, see my example in the exercises at the end of this chapter.

My Overview Strategic Plan Table

PRIORITY	Goal	Getting There	Current Status	Obstacles	Resources	Allies	Next Step	Payoff
1								
2								
3								
4								

Recap

Here is a quick review to boost your energy and maintain focus. To set your goals and plan your strategy, you need to:

- Make a SPICE list.
- Separate realistic from unrealistic goals.
- Prioritize your goals on a short list.
- Fill in your strategic plan table.

Still need some more help? The exercises at the end of this chapter can help you figure out your training path. If you're all set, great! Move on to the next chapter. For more information about constructing your table, move on to the exercises below.

Exercise 1 will help you to set up your own Strategic Plan Table noting your current or future goals/objectives. Use my examples as a guide if you want.

Exercise 2 asks you to take a look at your long-term objectives as a way to clarify today's strategic plan. Sometimes our future goals can really refresh our thinking about today. Try setting up five- and ten-year plans by yourself or with your partner. Of course, your plans will evolve and change over time, but it is good to know if someone has a desire to move to another area of the country, be closer to family, change jobs or careers, or even have special vacation trips in mind.

EXERCISES

Warm Up: Reflective Stretches

Taking Down Obstacles

Using your SPICE list from Chapter 1, write down what is stopping you from bringing some of the lifelong values, goals, and/or interests into your life now. Use the **Overview Strategic Plan Table** below to guide you from your objective to your next step. Create your own table or use the one provided for you within this chapter and fill in the steps. If you need clarity regarding definitions, re-read "Filling Out Your Overview Strategic Plan Table" in this chapter.

Be honest with yourself about what is blocking you or burdening you. If fear is one of your obstacles, write your fears down! You can often break fear down and defeat it once you identify its source. Fear of success or of failure can easily be an obstacle. Fear of making a fool of oneself (pride) is another common one. Fear of the unknown or of not knowing how to tackle a project is also very common.

Overview Strategic Plan Table (My example from Aug. 2004)

PRIORITY	Goal	Getting There	Current Status	Obstacles	Resources	Allies	Next Step	Payoff
1	To establish new career from writing and workshops	Write and publish The Sport of Motherhood	Partial success: need to finish workbook, manuscript, and begin focus groups and workshops. Have self-discipline down	Impatience; fear that I won't be able to do it; time—always interrupted, not enough time	Books, writing, running, prayer, affirmations, prayer group	Spouse, family friends, Dream Team, writing group	Break goals down, one step at a time. Pray daily for courage, perseverance and insight. Utilize "Dream Team" for accountability	Professional development, financial independence, connection with pre-kid self
2	To be less of a people-pleaser mentally	Utilize Strategic Plan to help set boundaries	Do pretty well unless it is about taking on a new commitment	Don't want to say no and let person who asked down	Playgroups and reality checks among friends, writing, books, meetings, prayer	Spouse, friends	Affirm what I can do, who I am. Remind myself that others get to enjoy things I pass up	More relaxed, not stressed; more confidence
3	To pace myself better during the week	Schedule downtime!	Partial success: I pace for marathons but tend to be more of a sprinter during week	Hard to give myself a break but getting better about it; need to edit more	Running, writing	Prayer group, spouse, family, friends	Build downtime into my weekly schedule	More energy and balance; better health

28   THE SPORT OF MOTHERHOOD

PRIORITY	Goal	Getting There	Current Status	Obstacles	Resources	Allies	Next Step	Payoff
4	To have less clutter in my life	One step at a time	Getting there: understand the need to de-clutter and do so now every week. Too much stuff makes me feel claustrophobic.	Small children who create clutter all of the time; too many papers; very little space (small house)	Books, magazine articles, playground chats	Moms of small kids who are in the same boat; spouse	De-clutter house at least 1 hr. per week and car every day; continue training children to organize and put away things	Peace of mind; content with what I/we already have
5	To feel more connected to other adults	Continue programs already in place (Mom's Night Out or MNO, Playgroups, etc.); continue to accept invites out; utilize sitter	Pretty successful but must be mindful of need to schedule time with adult friends	Can barely carry on an adult conversation due to multiple needs of kids; do not have many opportunities to talk to adult friends on phone or during	Mom's Night Out events (hard to get there but always feel better once I am there). Runs, walks, or coffee with friends	MNO, friends, writing group, Dream Team	Continue to reach out when feel disconnected—can even be a phone call	Social stimulation; feel more a part of; better mothering because happier

Practice: New Skills

Taking the Long View

Sometimes considering the future helps you jump-start action today. Write up a five- or ten-year plan with your partner.

1. Have your partner write down his or her values and goals (re-read list of values in Chapter 1 Exercises for ideas if necessary). Compare them with your list. What are the similarities between your lists? What are the differences?

2. Write down three things that you would each like the other to change, improve, do, or not do. Talk about how you can help each other with this.

3. If moving could be part of your future plan, come up with possible locations together.

4. Write down families that you like doing things with, even on a quarterly or biannual basis.

5. Write down quarterly goals together, and make purposeful commitments. (Get together with other couples once or twice a quarter. Set up a regular date night that both partners can count on. List some ideas for fun parent dates. List some ideas for fun family outings. Address budget goals. Address time management goals. Establish a weekly game night with kids and spouse. . ..)

Cool Down

1. Where can you edit? (Too many commitments, boards, activities, parties or play dates? Too much spending? If so, where can you cut?)

2. List possible vacations and then create a hierarchy with the most fabulous first. Put your favorites on a five-year map.

CHAPTER 3

Teamwork at Home

> ▶ R U a pack horse on a daily basis?
> ▶ R U looking 4 ideas 2 help motivate the kids (or your partner) 2 do chores?
> ▶ How about developing a game plan at home that can help U + your partner make decisions quickly?

Though running can be a solitary sport, a runner with a good support team gets a big boost from her team's help and encouragement. She finds that her training and her races are easier, more fun, and more exciting. For running moms, making time for workouts and races often involves coordinating with her partner to arrange child care, meals, carpools, and shopping. For any mom, a support network is essential. Teamwork at home is *the* critical part of your support network. So get ready to set up your home-based support team.

If everyone at home pulls some weight, you will have more energy and time to do fun things with your family. A helpful, supportive partner is a treasure. Jill, a working mom of two, says, "I have a very supportive husband. Chores are shared equally. My children have known since weaning that Dad can do almost anything Mom can do."

Teamwork at home includes all members of the extended family team including parents and in-laws, aunts and uncles, cousins, and other relatives. Many moms depend on various members of their extended families to help out, particularly if both the mother and father are working and struggling to make ends meet. There are also many moms who can afford to hire help such as nannies, babysitters, au pairs and housekeepers. Paid help is more common with two-career families in major urban markets such as New York City, Boston, Chicago, and San Francisco.

Having a teamwork plan at home enables you to work on your own strategic plan. Your partner's help, or a relative's help, can make a big difference. Children can help, too. This chapter focuses on laying a foundation for teamwork at home. It introduces a philosophy of parenting that values helpfulness and that teaches pitching in, divvying up chores, and sharing work and rewards. Work through this chapter to put a similar philosophy in place and, almost before you know it, you'll have a family of team players.

Philosophy of Parenting: A Game Plan

When I was a high school English teacher, I developed a concrete philosophy of teaching based on consistency and clarity. In my classrooms, I saw that my students thrived in a structured environment, knowing what was expected and where the limits were. My teaching career made me a better parent because what was true of my students turned out to be true of my children, too: They thrive in a supportive, structured environment. I also realized that I wasn't doing a student any favors when I extended a deadline for him or her. More likely, I was encouraging bad habits that would make things harder for that student in the long run. What would play in the back of that student's head the next time a deadline approached? The alluring idea that the deadline would be extended if he or she just played the story right. Over and over again, I had the same students asking for extensions. The students had gotten into the bad habit of trying to work the system. One thing I learned from teaching and parenting is that kids *always* remember when you make an exception to the rule. If you are inconsistent, they notice and they remember. Instead of getting on task, the student or child asks, "But what about the time when. . . ?" Have you heard that one before?

A philosophy of parenting will help you establish values and priorities that you can apply both to your overall family life and to the daily business of childrearing. With a philosophy of parenting in mind, you can pick and choose your battles with your children. You won't get caught up in every scuffle or disagreement. Your kids will still enjoy being kids while they learn your family's ground rules. In fact, your steady guidance enhances their childhood! For example, in our house, respect towards self and others carries greater weight than "dawdling."

My husband and I created a philosophy of parenting based on our core values and expectations:

1. We want to raise children who are honest, kind, and respectful towards themselves and others.
2. We want them to practice the Golden Rule: "Do unto others as you would have them do unto you."
3. Ultimately, we hope to put ourselves "out of business" as parents by raising our children all the way up in a loving, faith-based household. We look forward to knowing them as adults who honor the values we taught them.

When we are faced with a need to make a quick decision, we can always go back to **our philosophy of parenting**; it is our manual for how to make a decision when we are on the move or under pressure. Our philosophy involves **consistency** (pick a few rules and stand by them), **limits** (clear and reasonable), and **accountability** (if you choose to break a rule, then you choose to accept the consequence). Our children find plenty of freedom within those guidelines, and they also enjoy the enormous comfort that comes from expected structure and routines.

Our main goal as parents is to raise good citizens, so we know that we have to teach them self-respect and respect for others. We also know that, when they are grown, we will have to send them off into the world on their own. All along the way, we keep an eye on these goals but we try not to take ourselves too seriously.

Walter Barry, a father of three who was on cable TV's *The Sport of Motherhood* Show, says good parenting involves having "strong marital DNA with your spouse." In other words, it requires "a common set of values and ideals, unconditional love for each other, and an awareness of each other's weaknesses, which includes supporting each other's goals and passions." By giving each other room to grow, you are keeping the spark in a marriage.

> ## DAD TIP
> Walter and his wife Cecile have a "short list of things" that they keep in mind:
> 1. Be a team player
> 2. Love your family and your friends
> 3. Love to learn
> 4. Take ownership in your life as much as you can
> 5. Always do the right thing
> 6. Be who you are; express your feelings

I have heard so much practical wisdom about parenting in my *Sport of Motherhood* workshops and in interviews with parents. But parents themselves—immersed in raising kids, earning money, driving, cleaning, and shopping—seldom have the time to think about their everyday parenting as a philosophy. Maybe it seems more like a circus. But if you sit down and articulate your parenting values, you may well find that you have the beginning of a strong philosophy in place. Here are some examples of specific ideas from my workshops and interviews. It's inspiring to read them!

- **Allowing Mistakes** — "Allow your children to learn from common mistakes. Sometimes we feel like a failure if our children are not perfect; however, those teachable moments are crucial to the normal development of all individuals." (Chris)

- **Accepting the Strengths and Limitations of Your Own Children** — "I am learning to accept who my children are and to work with that. Letting them be [sic] who they are." (Carlita)

- **Setting Boundaries and Expectations** — "My parenting philosophy is to be honest and loving and to set firm, reasonable boundaries." (Robbie)

- **Being Loving and Intentional** — "Love 'em to pieces and cherish every developmental stage. Make sure to inculcate politeness and safety; don't sweat much else. Talk to them as responsible, mature people. Bolster their self-confidence by appreciating and noticing all the progress that happens—verbal, small motor, large motor, social, moral. Give small hints of ways to improve without getting on their backs." (Simone)

- **Teaching Tolerance** — "My children are taught that all people are equal and they should never look at the color of someone's skin to make judgments about whether or not to make friends with them. It is okay to notice differences as long as they are in passing. The really important things are what draw the two spirits together." (Chris)
- **Teaching Honesty** — "I believe that honesty is the key to a successful parent-child relationship." (Martha)

> **MOM TIP**
>
> "White lies are sometimes as dangerous as more hurtful lies. I am very strict about lying. If I know that something happened and I have to work hard to find out the truth, the punishment is always more severe than when I am told right up front. Teachable moments are wonderful tools but not if I am exhausted from having to dig for the truth." —Chris

- **Doing Your Best and Being a Team** — "Do my best, know I will not get everything I want to done in a day, allow time for myself (the gym, needlepoint, night out with a friend) and also work together with my husband. He and I are a team. Give him attention, affection and appreciation. It makes a world of difference!! Don't argue with him in front of the children. Present a united front." (Linda)
- **Evolving Needs** — "[Our parenting] evolves and changes as we as parents grow and change.

> **Mom Story**
>
> "My overarching philosophy is that women live their lives in chapters. This chapter is not the one where I will work, read the paper or learn to really garden. There will be other chapters when I do those things. That has allowed me to be much less frustrated and resentful about being a stay-at-home mother."
> —Dana

It centers around doing what feels right for our family at the time. It entails being present for our children's needs (physical, emotional, spiritual, and intellectual). We strive to have children who are respectful, honest, empathetic and caring." (Anita)

- **Keeping Perspective** — "My favorite [mini] philosophy is to pick my battles. I agree in theory, but it is awfully hard for me to let the little things slide. . . ." (Dana)

Now that you have read through these examples, begin writing down ideas for your philosophy of parenting. This is not meant to be an intimidating task. It's a simple game plan that can save you time and energy when faced with a need for quick decisions. You can create your unique philosophy of parenting by:

1. Picking three or four values that you want your children to have. (See the exercises at the end of the chapter if you'd like to look at a list of values to jog your memory.)
2. Creating a few rules and ways to stick to them. The values can guide the rule-making.
3. Establishing appropriate consequences for broken rules. It's great to have these in place ahead of time because you know the rules are probably going to be broken at some point.

Write out a statement that addresses these goals and objectives and is easy to remember. Keep it brief. Use three to four sentences at most. This is the framework for your philosophy of parenting. (More step-by-step instructions are in the chapter exercises.)

Your philosophy of parenting is *yours*. You can gather ideas from others, but ultimately you and your partner need to hammer out the priorities and set up your game plan. Ideally, you support each other in front of the kids and discuss any necessary fine-tuning away from them so that you don't undermine each other's authority. You are a team, and you don't want the kids playing you against each other.

Cheryl, a mom of teenagers, advises parents to work on partnership tools and develop a united front while their kids are young. When you are practiced at working together, you can plan ahead. Discuss your opinions on hot topics, such as body piercing and tattoos, well before your kids hit the age when those issues can arise. How do you feel about paying kids an allowance? About teens dating? Getting summer jobs? Using the family car? Figure out where you stand and whether or not you are on the same page. Cheryl tells parents "do it [your talking] now and you can be more prepared for when your teenagers target the chinks in your marital walls" to get what they want. Do it now and keep your marriage alive and healthy, because many marriages are strained or fall apart when the kids are teenagers. You can prevent that strain by planning ahead. With a strong, consistent parenting philosophy in their lives, teenagers can be some of the best, most energizing family team members.

Sharing the Load: Chores, Routines, and Expectations

Below are some tips and tools for fostering teamwork gleaned from different modern mothers. Keep in mind that what works for one person may not work for another person, or another family. Try some ideas out for fun. Toss the ones that don't work for you. What can you lose?

1. Train your kids early on to help you with the household responsibilities.

You are doing your kids a favor by helping them to establish practical habits that prepare them for the real world. Begin early on by asking them to help with easier chores like setting the table, folding and putting away laundry, picking up their rooms, and making their beds. Later you can move on to taking out trash, feeding pets, making their own school lunches, and doing their own laundry. Praise, sticker charts and allowance are all ways to affirm the teamwork and create routines.

> ### MOM TIP
>
> If you have trouble getting younger kids to pick up, you can read them *The Berenstain Bears and the Messy Room* by Stan and Jan Berenstain. Since the bear cubs are having trouble staying on task with cleaning up their toys, Mama Bear puts the toys remaining on the floor in a big collection box. Since they haven't been picked up, she will give them away. This collection box really motivates kids to take ownership of their toys and favorite clothes. Some moms do this and put the box in the garage. If kids forget about the toys and don't ask for them for over a week, then they give them to Goodwill.

2. Turn work into play by making up games as you work together on a task.

Sometimes a "five-minute pickup" race is all anyone needs for a morale booster. Set a timer and see how much everyone can accomplish in five or ten minutes. Sing songs while you clean up. The Barney "Clean-Up" song is always a favorite with the younger set: "Clean up, clean up, everybody does their share. Clean up, clean up, everybody everywhere." Try different tunes, sing faster, then slower, quieter and then louder. Work doesn't have to be boring.

To occupy school-age kids while you are doing a more rigorous cleaning, fill a bowl with strips of paper. Draw or write one chore per paper. Some examples are: clean the window with a spritzer of water and a paper towel; sweep the kitchen floor; clean the bathroom floor with a mop; use a mini-vacuum on the couch; organize a drawer or toy box. A child can pick one strip, which you or an older sibling can read to her, finish that chore, then come back for another.

Marian, a working mother of two, tapes the strips to one side of the window. After her girls pick a chore and do it, they move their strips of paper to the other side of the window. Kids make a lot of clutter, so teach them that they can also help control it. Every year or so, have the five-and-older set test markers or pens and throw out the old ones. Ask them to go through their socks and weed those that are too worn or too small. Kids feel empowered when given these small decisions, and they are learning to make sound judgments at the same time.

3. Train your kids to help you with loading or unloading the car.

Ever notice how, at the end of a fun day-trip or visit, everyone jumps out of the car and charges into the house, leaving you with all the tag ends of their day? Crumpled papers, books, a stray flip-flop. I taught my kids to ask, "How can I help you, Mom?" whenever we are setting off in the car and when we get home. Initially, I explained to them that we simply could not go to as many places if I didn't have their help because I would be bogged down figuring out who needed what, gathering all of the gear, and then keeping track of it. Too many to-dos for Mom, too much time and energy wasted.

We are a team. If we do the work together, we have more time to do the fun things together. I am so obviously happy when they ask, "How can I help you, Mom?" that I usually don't have to remind them. It has become a fun game for them to see who remembers to say it first. Of course I always say, "Thaaaaaaaaaaaank you!" with a big smile and off we go. We backtrack and re-do things if they forget. Children learn to do by helping. If you take every task on yourself, they will not learn the value of their help.

Do my kids always do this? No way! We are all a work in progress.

4. Teach your children that actions have consequences.

This is one of your most portable and handy tools: keep consistent rules that have reasonable consequences. If you go to the park, and one of your children begins misbehaving, explain to the child that if she or he is too tired to behave well, you'll all just have to go home. Although siblings may complain that it's unfair to end their fun early, remind them that it's your rule to get a tired, cranky child home for rest. If someone isn't behaving, he or she must be tired, and that means it's time to go. Kids quickly get the picture and—being very resourceful—help to keep the errant child on track.

If you do have to go home from the park (or another outing) early, try to do something special with the kids who were behaving. Give them some bonus television or computer time, read with them, or let them help choose and make dinner. Often it's your older kids in this situation just because they have more self-control and stamina. It's natural for them to be disappointed, and it's OK to make it up to them in little ways. They'll appreciate that you are acknowledging their good behavior, and that will go a long, long way toward erasing their disappointment. And it shows them that their good behavior did have a good consequence!

That's not to say that older kids don't get tired, cranky, rude, and hard to get along with. My oldest two sometimes get into he-said/she-said battles when they are tired. This usually happens after a very busy day, often when I'm tired as well. I encourage them to work this out themselves, keeping an ear open to make sure things don't get out of hand. Sometimes they just need to be separated from each other for a short while or get a bit of exercise. This is a next step for them in learning consequences. These negotiation skills will prove invaluable in later years.

5. Figure out what works for your family and your dynamic.

Whatever tasks you are asking your children to do, give some thought to setting up a system that really works for your family and schedule. Take laundry as an example. Each child can have his or her own laundry day so that the machines are empty and ready. Or Sunday can be kids' laundry day so everyone is working together. One of the kids could wash and fold all their towels while the other strips their beds and washes and folds their sheets. Kids can fold large sheets together—that takes real teamwork! You can make laundry easier on little ones by getting them their own mesh sock bags that go directly into the washer and dryer and then back into their drawers.

Sachi Itagaki, a guest on *The Sport of Motherhood* TV Show, discusses her laundry system. She and her husband share doing the loads. When a load is dry, she dumps the laundry in a pile in the living room. Everyone is responsible for sorting their own laundry and putting it away in drawers and closets. "I don't care how it is put away so long as it leaves the living room and doesn't go onto someone's bedroom floor!" This system works well for Sachi's family.

Housework, like all kinds of work, often carries bigger issues and messages. Carlita says that one day she caught her youngest saying, "This is women's work" as he was stuffing clothes into the washer. This triggered her to teach her boys to value the work of a stay-at-home mom. "I tell the children about my day so that they can see what a stay-at-home mom does. They are also responsible now for doing all of their own laundry. I only buy colored clothing, and they can put it all in the washer. They separate the shirts, spray Simple Green on the stains, fold and sort and put away." Now Carlita and her boys have a good system going.

Maybe you do the wash and have the kids help fold, sort and put away their clothes. If you can't stand wrinkles and want to fold or iron, then teach the kids to load the clothes and turn on the washer. Do what works, but definitely involve them. One day they will need to be responsible for their own laundry. If they are used to helping out now, they won't find it hard to manage later. Something will work! Stick with it; ride out the bumps as you experiment and find your system.

6. Training takes time but the payoff is worth it.

When two of my children were ages seven and five, we had them taking out the trash and recycling. At first, the whole process took about thirty minutes. Now they are used to their weekly trips "to the Land of Stinky," as they like to call it, and they can do the job in about fifteen minutes.

> **MOM TIP**
>
> Raise the standards as your children get older. Expect children to do a job well. A three-year-old can probably not make the bed as well as a nine-year-old, though you might be surprised. If the nine-year-old does a sloppy job, then ask him or her to re-do it. The idea is not to create more work, but to teach them to do something well once. I remind mine of the cost involved in re-doing chores. Lost time, lost energy, and Mom and Dad's lost patience are all costs they pay when a chore isn't done right.

Interested in more tips for creative and practical ways to get children to share the load? Look at *Marguerite Kelly's Family Almanac: A Helpful Guide to Navigating Through the Everyday Issues of Modern Life* by Marguerite Kelly and Katy Kelly or visit www.organizedhome.com for concrete and manageable to-do lists and tips. Elaine St. James' *Simplify Your Life with Kids: 100 Ways to Make Family Life Easier and More Fun* is filled with practical advice ranging from simple discipline strategies to making the time to enjoy your family. You can also do a Google search on the Internet using "children and chores" as the keywords. There are plenty more strategies available.

Dads as Team Players

With the changing face of the American family, dads are pitching in more than ever before with childrearing and household responsibilities. More dads are sharing childcare with their wives so that both can work. Parents arrange flextime schedules to stagger their working and parenting hours. Dierdra, a working mother of two, thinks that "by getting involved, dads feel like their children are connecting with them and coming to them." At first, her husband worried about the flextime schedule, which involved staggering hours and shifting things around at home and at work, because he "felt like he was under a microscope. But his supervisor had a couple of young kids. . . . People are more understanding now of men needing to put their families at a greater priority than ever before."

People in managerial positions are also more aware that employees may need flexible schedules since more women and men are working part time. Dierdra sums it up nicely: "Husbands are not only coming home to change diapers. They are also altering their hours or schedule to play a bigger part in raising their children and to support wives who seek more fulfillment."

Many dads are adapting their work schedules to their family's needs. Some dads get to work before dawn to that they can coach kids' sports, lead Scouts, or participate in the PTA. A few years ago, my son needed a little extra TLC, so my husband met him after school once a week to play wall ball or foursquare or throw a football. All I had to do was ask. (What a great family tradition this started. Now that my son is older, he actively seeks more one-on-one time with his father, and he and "Dad" play tennis together a couple of times a week.) When my writing schedule cranked up, my husband began pitching in by making more trips to Costco, cooking dinner, and doing laundry.

Chris summarizes how essential it is for Dad and Mom to be a successful team. "It is important to show a united front with your partner when dealing with a situation with a child. If the child feels that there is some way to break the union on the issue, the parents have already lost. Children feel safe when rules are imposed and like it when we check up on their stories, even if they don't show it."

> **Mom Story**
>
> Mary Ann describes ways that her husband contributes positive energy to their team at home. She says that he "is an amazing dad and husband. I have learned so much from him. How he approaches a problem and situation and how he honors me as a wife and a friend, how he gives me space to figure things out. He does not come down hard on me. I feel like we are in this together. When I am struggling with things, he is not a big critic. He is easygoing and makes me more that way. He is a powerful influence in a quiet, understated way."

What About Dads Who AREN'T Team Players?

In both *The Sport of Motherhood* Workshops and in "Dear Genevieve" advice column letters, I often hear the following question: But what if your husband doesn't help out, or has to be nagged to do it or is unwilling to change? Some questions indicate that a mom doesn't feel respected for the work she does in the home. In this sort of case, the husband actually does have the potential to change. Other questions brought up the issue of cultural barriers. When I interviewed moms about how they experienced these cultural differences, many of them wrote about finding alternative solutions or work-arounds. We can learn a lot from their experiences, so I have included three of the advice column questions below:

> Dear Genevieve,
>
> I sometimes feel resentful towards my husband because he refers to his work outside the home as a "real job" and what I do at home as easy and fun. I do love what I get to do—stay home with my kids. And I know he can't do what I do. So challenging him to take my job for a week would just make more work for me—and one day wouldn't make him understand. But how do I help him to understand that I feel demeaned and disrespected? I want both of us to feel that I am his equal partner in our marriage and family life and that I am hardworking and indispensable.
>
> Signed,
> *"Just a Mommy"*
> Palo Alto, CA

Dear Just a Mommy,

Just so you know, you are not alone. Many couples have to address these issues, especially around the births of new children or career changes. It sounds like you two are ready for a talk about teamwork. Together you create the solid base upon which your family can stand.

We get to make choices in our marriages. How we choose to talk to each other. How we want our marriages to play out. If one person does not feel valued, she can set the tone in the home for the whole family. The old saying, "If mama isn't happy, nobody's happy," has a lot of truth to it!

Here are some tips you can try to lighten your load and get you back on course. Talk openly about how you can support each other and the kind of language that needs to be used. Maybe your husband is not aware of how he's saying things to you. Does he give the message that he supports you and values the work you do in front of the children? Let him know that they will pick up on his signals. Remind him that people who are good at what they do can make anything look easy. Maybe he also needs you to tell him how much you value what he does.

Show him your mom marathon training schedule. Try writing down your daily to-do list, including loads of laundry, dishes and snack and meal prep, so that he and the kids can see what you do each day. This can help him if you are sick or away. Go out with your girlfriends for a day and let him have the kids, the responsibilities, and the household. He can enjoy the time with the kids and gain some more appreciation for what you do each day. You get to design and travel this course together, but sometimes you need to nudge each other to get on the same path.

Sincerely,
Genevieve

How do I get my husband to help out with the kids and the household more without sounding resentful or nagging? There is always so much picking up to do and I feel like I am going in circles.

Signed,
Looking for Some Ideas
Palo Alto, CA

Dear Looking for Some Ideas,

Teamwork at home frees up time to enjoy each other more. You can start by getting your kids on board with helping out around the house. Though it takes time to train them to set and clear the table, unload the groceries and take out the recycling, you are doing both them and yourself a favor. They are learning to be helpful, responsible individuals. Ask your husband to help train them, too and, of course, he can help by example.

Humor is also a great way to make a point. I remember when I got tired of seeing dishes in the sink. I told my husband, "Hey, did you know that we don't have Dish Fairies living here?" He laughed. Another time he joked with me and asked, "Do you think when you turn 40 you might learn how to put the paper towel roll on the holder?" It worked!

After some quiet time together when the kids are in bed, ask each other what might be helpful. For example, one mom said that she wants her husband to ask her how he can help when he gets home from work. So he does. She also asked him what he needs or would like. He wants 10 to 15 minutes to go through the mail and read the paper when he comes home, and then he can transition into a helpful family man.

You don't have to run this course alone. A little bit of teamwork and support can go a long way.

Sincerely,
Genevieve

Dear Genevieve,

I'm getting tired. I work full time and run the house and "run" the kids. I am den mother to my son's Cub Scouts, co-leader to my daughter's Girl Scouts and keep up a hectic soccer schedule during most of the year. Every weekend I'm delivering the kids here or delivering the kids there. My husband comes from a different culture than mine, and though he participates in other ways this does not include much time with the kids. My son is getting old enough that I feel his Cub Scouts should have a more male role. My husband has rarely seen my son play soccer because it conflicts with his own soccer time. I can't remember the last time I did something just for me or even time alone with my husband. It's go, go, go. This was OK at first but I've been doing things this way for years now. How can I get my husband to pick up the ways of the Western dads?

Signed,
One-sided
Princeton, NJ

Dear One-sided,

I interviewed several moms with a similar bicultural marital dynamic. Here is what worked for three of them:

Mom #1 created a positive scenario. She "began with fake praises." Instead of criticizing her husband, she praised him for what she wanted him to do in front of the kids and played up what he actually did do. She "wanted the kids to have a positive, not a negative, picture. He then wanted the kids to think of him that way and slowly changed. It worked." She is very happy with the situation now.

Mom #2, a university professor, saw the situation was not going to change and outsourced for help. "Since he's busy and I'm busy, I got professional help: a full-time housekeeper and babysitter. Otherwise, I cannot work."

Mom #3 understands the situation won't change, so she and her husband are planning to draw on extended family support. "He watched our toddler for a day and understood the amount of work involved. He also doesn't want to take it on." They are currently discussing a move to be near her family so that

> she can get the help and support she needs, and possibly go back to work part time.
>
> These are tips from moms in the trenches. Take what you need and leave the rest. Ask other moms how they do it. You'd be surprised to find out how easily moms want to share what has worked for them.
>
> Sincerely,
> *Genevieve*

Some Helpful Partnership Tools

I have collected partnership tools from numerous women who have shared what works for them in their marriages. Try not to get overwhelmed by all of the possibilities. This is not a to-do list! Use this list as a springboard to get to your own ideas or focus on one or two that appeal to you. Remember, we all struggle with these issues at one time or another—or all at once!

- Use Your Philosophy of Parenting. Create a philosophy of parenting if you have not already done so. It will give a shape to your game plan. Together, clarify your values and objectives for the family. Pick your battles, and try to agree upon consistent consequences.

- Identify Priorities and Primary Responsibilities. Whether they are staying at home or working, mothers today are busier than ever. Clear communication about duties and responsibilities becomes critical. We do a lot of juggling. For some of us, creating a working partnership is about identifying which balls we could drop to preserve our sanity.

Mom Tip

Letting go of familial or cultural expectations can help. You get to make up the rules in your nuclear family. Maybe the house is a little messier than the one you lived in growing up. "Maybe you do not have the time or desire to cook elaborate dinners like your mother. Share what you can, hire a cleaner every two weeks, or let some of it go. You have different responsibilities than your mother did." —Karen

- **Get Organized.**
    1. Create a Daily Family Schedule. Write up routines and time estimates for school mornings, after school, and bedtime. Be specific. You can use pictures for smaller kids. A daily schedule works to center the family. Everyone is on the same page and knows what to do—even the sitter!
    2. Pick one night a week to sit down with your partner and go over schedules. If you want, you can merge calendars either electronically or by hand. Which nights are family dinner nights? What is on the calendar for the weekend? How can you edit your schedules?
    3. Keep your family calendar ready. You can use different highlighter colors for different activities or people so that even the youngest can interpret the color-coded schedule and know what the day brings.
- **Make Your Needs Known.** Trust me, most people cannot read your mind. If you do not let people know what you need, you can't hold them responsible for disappointing your hopes. If you would like for your husband to join you at a parent education talk, ask him to be there and let him know that it needs to be a priority. Letting family members know why particular things are important to you will help them to better understand your requests.
- **Recognize That Your Way Is Not the Only Way.** Be open to other ways of doing things. Chris sums it up: "In the parenting partnership with my husband, I have had to step back and let his parenting personality come out. I tend to repeat to myself, 'It's not

the way I would have done it, but [insert child's name] has come through it okay.'" Be flexible.

- **Establish Boundaries.** Draw them around your nuclear family. You and your partner are a team first. For example, an alliance between you and your mother over your husband can muddy the marriage waters and confuse the kids.

- **Listen.** Put your agenda aside so that you can actively listen to your partner. Try to pick a good time to talk, a time when he can be a good audience. Maybe an ideal time is when he is shaving or engaged in something relaxing!

- **Be Respectful Towards Your Partner.** It matters. Show it, speak it, act it, and your children will follow your model.

- **Use Humor to Get a Point Across.** Remember my examples: "FYI, there aren't any dish fairies living here." My husband has teased me by remarking hopefully that "one day you, too, will learn to put the paper towel roll on the dispenser." Humor reminds us that no one is perfect. In fact, our small imperfections are part of our charm. Laugh about them, and it's easier to improve.

- **Give and Take.** If your partner is tired from a late night at work, pushing hard for deadlines, or even has a lingering cold, he might want to cancel out of a family plan, like attending that parent education talk. If it's a very important event to you, offer to help find him some extra downtime the next day or on the weekend. Can you do something to help him recharge? Give and take. No strings attached.

- **Offer Choices.** Being offered a choice is almost like getting an invitation! For example, ask, "Would you like to put the kids to bed or do the dinner dishes?" By offering a choice, you also remind everyone that there is plenty to do.

By the way, this works well with kids, too, and can be very funny. One mom always makes one of the options the same unsavory task. She asks, "Would you like to unload the dishwasher or do dog-doo pickup?" "Would you like to clean out the car or do dog-doo pick up?" Her kids jump on the choice! Finally one laughed, "Would I like to grow up or do dog-doo pickup?"

- **Be Loving.** Say "I love you," or find something nice to say to your partner every day.
- **Don't Say What You Don't Mean.** You may be madder than a hornet one minute, but don't say hurtful things just to get a jab in. Words do matter and are remembered even after you make up.
- **Don't Let Things Fester.** Although it is unwise to speak in haste when you are angry, it is also unwise to wait too long before bringing something to your partner's attention. Even if it seems silly, if it is bothering you, then it is important to share.
- **Don't Criticize or Make Fun of Your Partner in Front of Others.** You are a team. Don't you want to stay happily married? It also makes others around you uncomfortable. If you have something to say, pull your spouse aside and share it privately. More likely than not, the information will be better received.
- **Support Each Other.** Keep the dreams alive. Encourage and support each other's personal growth.
- **What if He is Preoccupied, Can't, or Won't Hear You?** Call him on it. Spell it out—nicely. This one works well, but use it sparingly: "If you don't have time to talk right now, I can go pay a therapist so that I can talk about [the issue]." Tell him about your priorities. Give him the information so that you do not build up resentments.
- **Make Time Just for the Two of You.** Yes, the logistics involved can exhaust you, but this is important. Keep your marriage alive and healthy.

> **MOM TIP**
>
> "Set up regular date nights. Get away for an overnight or a week. Remember why you fell in love with each other." —Clara

We all know that a relationship can take some work. Overall, respect for each other is the root of a strong partnership. As the children get older and the family busier, sometimes we have to be more insistent, even stubborn, about creating the time to work on our partnerships. Try to address things as they come up. Clear the air as you move along in your week. Think of it as short-term pain, long-term gain. This frees you up to keep the play and laughter alive and well.

Take the time to say "hello" and "I love you." Schedule those date nights and keep the commitment. Treat your partner the way in which you want to be treated. If we want our children to learn about love, patience and respect, it is up to us to model that behavior for them. This not only teaches by example, but also helps to keep the flame in a marriage alive.

Wrap-Up

Your teamwork at home builds a solid base upon which you and your family can stand. By including children in chores at an early age, you are fostering self-reliance, independence and accountability. When you and your family work things out at home, negotiate, and share the load in a kind and loving way, you teach your children important interpersonal skills.

A philosophy of parenting offers guiding principles that set the tone in your home so that everyone thrives and feels loved and supported. By picking and choosing your battles with the kids, you can enjoy the family more, conserve energy, and find or keep some balance. When you and your partner work together to identify your personal goals both for today and for tomorrow, you are prepared to respect and encourage each other along your journeys. You have trained to be a team.

EXERCISES

Create a philosophy of parenting if you have not already done so. Get a game plan, clarify your values and objectives. Pick your battles and try to agree on consistent consequences. You can work on this with your partner, or work separately and then compare and discuss your responses.

Warm Up: Reflective Stretches

1. Do you like knowing the playing rules in a sport or in a work environment ahead of time?
2. Do you find yourself wondering how your partner or your mother would have handled a particular parenting situation?

3. Do you thrive in chaos or structure? What about your child(ren)?

Practice: New Skills

Pick three to five values that you want your child(ren) to have. I provide a list of suggestions below to prompt your thinking. Don't confine yourself to these. This exercise is all about defining *your* family's values.

> Attentive to Others, Balance, Charity, Compassion, Consideration, Contentment, Courage, Courtesy, Curiosity, Enthusiasm for Life/Learning, Fairness, Faith, Fortitude, Generosity, Graciousness, Gratitude, Growth in Grace, Heart for Missions, Honesty and Integrity, Hope, Humility, Joy, Justice, Kindness, Love, Loyalty, Mercy, Modesty, Openness, Peace-loving, Peacemaker, Perseverance, Prayerfulness, Prudence, Purity, Respect (for self, others, authority), Responsibility, Salvation, Self-Control, Self-Discipline, Thoughtfulness, Tolerance, Willingness and Ability to Work

Here's a simple example of a set of three values:

honesty
kindness
respect for self and others

Fill in these blanks with the values you have chosen, and have your partner do the same. What kind of overlap do you have? What is significant about each of your choices? Use this discussion to begin to establish your family values. If you are a single parent, you can do this on your own or include older children in the exercise.

1. _____   _____
2. _____   _____
3. _____   _____

Create a few rules and stand by them. Let the values you've identified guide the rule-making.

Rule 1: _____

Rule 2: _____

Rule 3: _____

Here's a list of examples to get you thinking about what your most important rules might be:

> The Golden Rule (treat others as you would want to be treated).
> Tell the truth.
> Show respect toward adults, authority figures, and others.
> Be a team player.
> Help out with chores.
> Take ownership in your life as much as you can.
> Take responsibility for your actions.
> Always do "the right thing."
> Give back to your community.

Once you have your rules in place, establish consequences for broken rules ahead of time (consequences should change with children's ages and stages).

Cool Down

List two rewards that motivate *you* to do your chores.

1. _____
2. _____

List two rewards involving family time that can motivate your kids to do their chores (examples: board games, movie night, special dinner, a trip or outing).

1. _____
2. _____

List two rewards that kids can do solo that motivates them to do chores on a weekly basis (examples: earn more computer time or phone time, get a new book or toy, or earn some allowance).

1. _____
2. _____

CHAPTER 4

Building a Personalized Support Network

> ▶ R U giving up on your goals before U really get started?
> ▶ R U interested N having a support network or shared interest group?
> ▶ Do U have accountability buddies, cheerleaders, + mentors N place 2 help U go the distance?

Runners use buddies, teams, and networking to enhance their training. Why? Group support improves their experience and their results. They feel better, run better, enjoy their training more. Mothers can do the same. You can build personalized support networks to meet your unique needs whatever they are: friendly camaraderie in an activity, focused support around a project, help with parenting tasks. Pretty much any need shines with support. Support networks come in all shapes and sizes, from a friend who shares your interests to an international organization, from a relaxed reading group to a formal support group for the parents of autistic children, from an online discussion group with thousands of members to your spouse. Whatever their shape or size, support groups can help you reach your goals.

Support networks can be informal or formal. Informal networks are spontaneous, while formal networks have a planned organization. Sometimes we overlook our informal support groups. When you meet a friend for a walk or a cup of coffee or when you visit with parents you regularly see at school, you are enjoying part of your support network. For example,

I met with three other elementary school mothers after morning drop-off at our kids' school. We gathered and talked about the journey to school that day. Relaxing with each other, we shared some of the challenges of the past twenty-four hours and discussed some strategies. Darice, a mother of three little ones, referred to our casual meeting as her "time to EXHALE." Chris, a working mother of two, said, "This is my only morning off from work. I needed this." We traded tips, got a dose of perspective and had a good belly laugh. Then we were ready to move on to our day. We had touched base, and we knew that we were not alone in this fun but crazy trip called motherhood.

Formal groups meet with a stated purpose, such as Mom's Night Out, a twelve-step meeting, a running or a writing group. Their purpose can include keeping members accountable, sharing ideas, sharing work (as in babysitting co-ops or carpools), planned activities, group study, and focused brainstorming. A formal group can be quite relaxed (a laid-back monthly reading group) or very focused (artists meeting to critique their work). Any formal group may also have several purposes. For example, a writing group offers accountability, encouragement, enrichment, and critique. Formal groups have a focus, such as parenting, writing, problem support, babysitting, or training for a race.

Another aspect of formal groups has to do with format. Unlike informal support groups (the moms who sometimes meet up at school drop-off), formal groups do have a format. How is the group structured? Its structure could be round robin, popcorn, lecture or discussion, online discussion, or email distribution. Each format has a different feel. In the round robin format, everyone takes a turn leading the group. You may find that group members are more enthusiastic and invested in a round robin group than in a group with a single designated leader. Perhaps the liveliest format is the popcorn format, which allows anyone to talk at anytime, but this format can be a problem if a few people dominate the discussion. Is it important for everyone to be physically present, or even virtually present, at the same time? If not, the online discussion format enables all participants to be involved at their own convenience since they can post their questions or answers at any time.

Mission statements can help a formal support group to define its purpose and get all group members on the same page. A group can hammer out a mission statement in the first couple of meetings. For example, I am part of a "Dream Team," which initially drew on Jack Canfield's book *The Power of Focus* as well as on his idea of creating a dream support group. Our mission statement: "To support, encourage, and aid group members in creating strategies for achieving their dreams through the consistent process of accountability and feedback." Our format: (1) Confirm date and time of next meeting and optional short discussion of assigned reading; (2) One member checks in regarding progress; (3) Group gives feedback; (4) That member writes down or discusses realistic and reachable goals for next meeting; (5) The next person checks in, and so on. Though we each have different career goals and paths, we support and push each other to break our goals down into manageable increments and to take our next steps. We also share relevant research on how to find a web builder, set up a business or company, and use the Internet for marketing. Our Dream Team has evolved into an "Entrepreneur Team," since we have moved from ideas to practice; we are all now starting or running our own businesses.

Rules, guidelines, and covenants can help to give a group structure and set expectations among group members. It's good to agree on these as the group gets going. Some group members may want to establish rules regarding attendance or productivity to hold the group to a higher standard. Others may balk at rules and prefer guidelines for some flexibility. Simple guidelines to govern speaking (sometimes called gatekeeper or timekeeper guidelines) can help group members use limited meeting time wisely. They also ensure that floor time for each speaker is allotted fairly and efficiently.

In larger groups, a predetermined procedure helps. For example, some groups proceed in alphabetical order or begin a meeting just where the previous meeting ended. It's a good idea to discuss these procedures at the first couple of meetings to see where everyone stands and move toward a consensus. In general, it's better to have fewer rules and guidelines, so as to not create a stifling atmosphere.

In more intimate groups, like prayer groups or even parent education support groups, group members sometimes agree to a covenant regarding things like confidentiality, attendance, and accountability. Regular attendance and a show of commitment are vital to smaller groups. If group members don't show up consistently, then the group is not an equal priority for all and cannot sustain itself.

Why Reach Out?

Being supported, connected, and encouraged can really boost your morale and help you go the distance. Support groups also give you an opportunity to share what you have learned and to help others. The multigenerational support that used to be available within families just isn't there for most women today, but mothers still need lots of help. We know this intellectually and physically. It's fairly easy to recognize that you cannot be in two places at one time, or to feel the deep exhaustion of trying to do it all alone. Nevertheless, it can be hard to take that first step—to reach out to others or to show up for the support group. Just do it.

> **MOM TIP**
>
> Use the **Triple Hitter Strategy**: Show up someplace three times and people begin to feel they know you. You look familiar. It takes time to form new connections, but the hardest part is starting. Give yourself time to settle in, such as five to ten meetings, before you assess whether the group is worthwhile for you.

Building Personalized Support Networks

The two keys to building your support networks are availability and compatibility. You need to find support that is both available—fits into your hectic schedule—and compatible—both willing and able to be there for you.

As you build or tailor a support network to meet some particular goal-related interest or need, consider whether some of your friends might be able to fill this role. One of the greatest challenges for moms is availability. We just aren't very available. Because of this, it makes sense for us to form our support network from among our existing friends, family, and acquaintances whenever possible. Let me give you an example. You have a friend that you meet to walk or run once a week, rain or shine. Could this friendship also include exercise accountability, since you already have an informal weekly commitment? Don't forget to make sure this friend is willing to be an accountability buddy. If both availability and compatibility match, then you know that Saturday morning runs with this friend will take care of a quota of exercise for the week and help keep you on track. Just make sure she doesn't feel burdened by your request; offer to do the same for her!

Not all of your friends and relationships need to be part of your support network. Support is just one of the aspects of friendship. If a friend doesn't fit in a particular support role, that doesn't mean that the friendship is weak or faulty. Almost all friends, being friends, provide support—in some cases it's just spontaneous or occasional. We all know that friend who disappears for months or even years, and then suddenly you're on the phone with her howling with laughter. That's priceless, but certainly not the place to look for a carpooling buddy. The first question to ask when considering someone as an ally is whether or not they can actively help you reach your goals.

> **Mom Story**
>
> You can even have parenting accountability buddies. Jackie, a working mother of two, talks about hers: "My friend calls me when she feels like she is being too hard on the kids and on herself. We keep each other in check. We need to get rid of the 'shoulds'."

Support Is a Two-Way Street

Why do some groups sustain themselves for years, while others fizzle out after a few meetings? Give and take within the group might be the most essential characteristic of healthy, long-running support groups. Participants have to be ready to give support as well as receive it. Sometimes your needs will be greater, but sometimes another group member may have a crisis that needs attention, and you'll be called upon to set your concerns aside for a moment and to offer up your help. The smaller the group, the more important the interplay among members will be. Be honest with yourself and the group about what you need and what you have to offer. We all have something to give. You don't have to be the group expert to listen carefully to another's problems and offer advice or encouragement.

Establish Solid Ground: Do a Friendship Assessment

Our friendships reveal a lot about who we are and who we want to be. Doing a Friendship Assessment will help you to step back, observe your friendships objectively, and describe the main role each friend plays in your life. Not all of your friends will be willing or able to be part of your active support network, but some will be delighted to help in this way and may ask the same of you.

Maybe you want quantity time with a friend, but she can only give you quality time. Maybe it is the other way around. Can you strike a balance? What can you do about your expectations? If you are aware of the mismatch, you can more easily address your feelings and put them in perspective. Mismatched expectations strain friendships and create stress. Identifying problems is the first step to their solution.

A Friendship Assessment can give you a healthy dose of awareness. Most friendships follow patterns, and the assessment will help you to recognize them. Which friendships boost your energy and which drain you? If a friendship is draining, maybe the realization will help you to change something and energize the relationship. Which friends need to see a lot of you (and feel lost if you aren't available) and which prefer to get together for briefer, more special occasions? You'll want to know which friendships are affected by parenting styles. As you build your personalized support system around your strategic plan, you can also identify cheerleaders, encouragers, and accountability buddies among your friends—or you'll notice the need for some of these types of people. Take five to ten minutes to fill in the following Friendship Assessment and learn some things about yourself and your current support base. So much of this is about compatibility and availability. Don't forget to include members from your immediate or extended family.

FRIENDSHIP ASSESSMENT AND AWARENESS

As we grow and change, so do our friendships. Ask the following questions about each of your friends. Use the table below to record your answers. Do it with as many friends as you can. Once you have finished the table, look it over and see what you can learn from it.

This is not meant to be callous assessment but a mindful awareness exercise.

- **Time** — Can you give Quality or Quantity time to this friend?
- **Time** — Does she/he seek Quality or Quantity time?
- **Time** — Can she/he give Quality or Quantity time to you?

- **Time** — Do you seek Quality or Quantity time with this friend?
- **Energy** — Does this friend add energy (make you feel good to just be around her or him) or drain energy?
- **Compatible or Incompatible Parenting Styles** — Or not applicable?
- **Stretch or Comfort** — Is she/he a stretch friend or comfort friend? The former tend to be very different from you, and being friends with them opens you up to different beliefs/viewpoints, while comfort friends tend to have the same values and beliefs you hold.
- **Positive or Negative** — Is this person a positive or negative influence on you? Positive = respectful, loving, kind, honest, and/or brings out the best in you. Negative = hurtful, dishonest, and/or you don't like how you behave when you are around this person.
- **Gold Brick** — Is this person a gold brick that you can put around your kids? Someone safe, loving, and wise to whom they can talk?
- **Fun and Funny** — Does this person make you laugh?
- **Ally** — Can this friend serve as an ally for goals in your strategic plan? Assign a specific role to each ally.
    - **A for Accountability Buddy** — Does she/he help keep you accountable to your goals? Often accountability involves just showing up.
    - **C for Cheerleader** — Does she/he encourage or support your goals? If someone believes in you, she/he can help you to take risks and grow.
    - **M for Mentor** — Is she/he a mentor at times or in certain areas of your life?

Friendship Assessment Table

	Name	Name	Name	Name	Name
Can you give Quality or Quantity Time?					
Does she seek Quality or Quantity Time?					
Can she give Quality or Quantity Time?					
Do you seek Quality or Quantity Time?					
Drain Energy or Energize?					
Compatible Parenting Style? (Yes, No, or N/A)					
Accountability Buddy?					
Encouraging, Supportive?					
Stretch or Comfort?					
Mentor in some area(s) of life?					
Positive or Negative Influence?					
Trigger Red Flags?					
Fun, Funny?					
Gold Brick?					
Ally for goals. List roles: A for Accountability, C for Cheerleader, or M for Mentor and pair with Goal. For ex., A, C/Exercise, M/Writing, or A/Prayer Work					
Potential ally for goals (List which goals)					

Did you miss any existing allies who could help with your strategic plan goals? If so, add them. If you find that a particular friend looks like the perfect ally, congratulations. That's a great discovery. But don't forget: always check with your friend before you assume she can be an active ally. You don't have to do this right away; wait for the right moment in the friendship and in your progress through your strategic plan.

Areas where you lack support are like holes in your Strategic Plan. Take a look at the table you constructed above to see where you lack support. Don't be surprised or worried if you can't complete your support network by relying on your friends. Most mothers need more than friends for support. Consider honestly whether you need to supplement the help your friends can give you with the "outside" help of a formal support group. If you are already hooked into one or more support groups, be sure to pick a few key people in those groups and run their names through the checklist as well. Do you have any holes or areas that lack support? It is now time to tailor those support networks to meet your currents needs or interests. Let's go.

Building Your Personalized Support Networks

There are three kinds of support networks: existing groups, new groups, and your current network of supporting friends and family. Since I addressed that personal network in the Friendship Assessment section, I will focus on the first two groups here.

You don't always have to build support groups from scratch. Sometimes they already exist. If a group already exists and you can join it, great! If the right group doesn't exist, then you may be looking at forming a new group.

Start your search for support by researching what is already available in your local community or in the various online communities. If the right group doesn't exist, then consider building a group from within your network of acquaintances, like school parents, church members, or others whom you already see on a regular basis. Don't forget your family either! Your spouse, siblings, parents, and even your older children can be a part of your support team.

Consider the type of support you need. Is this an area where you need to meet face-to-face or would an online discussion group suffice? Availability is always easier with electronic forums, but virtual support may not be what you need. Only you can determine what will work for you.

> **Mom Story**
>
> As you grow, your friendships may also change. Suzanne says, "Every now and then I assess priority friends vs. acquaintances." Robbie finds an assessment helpful also. "I have several close friends that I lean on regularly—they are simultaneously accountability buddies and cheerleaders. I also have several groups of friends—my AA friends, my preschool mom friends and my friends from growing up. They all give me different things. I also take stock of my friendships to determine which ones aren't working or what part of certain relationships isn't working. I have found that I need to let go of any friendship that is high-maintenance (person needs a lot of hand-holding) or emotionally draining."

A. Existing Groups: Finding Them and Joining Them

Once you have determined what you need, start to research what is available. Use the phone book, the local paper, city guides, local libraries, and community centers to find existing support groups and classes. Do a keyword search on Google and see what you get. There are many national organizations that have local chapters. You can speak with them on the phone, on the Internet, or in person at the local chapter.

Next let's explore the characteristics of some of the more common support groups. Seeing these groups through other moms' eyes may help you to decide what kind of group is right for you.

Mothers' Groups

The past decade has been tough on families. There have been so many job transitions, relocations, and upheavals that many women have become isolated and may struggle with a loss of identity as they mother young children or struggle with teen issues. Mothers' groups help women to connect, cope, and find or keep the joy of mothering. Some organize social outings and field trips for moms and kids, play groups, book groups, and even parenting education classes. Some mothers' groups are locally based in schools, towns and neighborhoods; others form around religious institutions or hospitals.

Arlene, a mother of three, talks about what led her to join a mothers' group. After a year of being a full-time working mom with long hours,

Arlene left a savvy career at an investment-banking firm to be home when her second child was born. She soon felt very out of sorts. Her husband was working long hours, and her friends—a network built during her early career—were also working. Meanwhile, she had her hands full with one and then two wonderful but demanding children. She slowly began to build a new network of mom friends, but she was very shy, so it was difficult.

When her family relocated, she found herself "overwhelmed and depressed." So she reached out and joined a local mothers' group. At one meeting, she identified with the speaker and during discussion time "just poured out my feelings for the first time. I told the group (of fifty or sixty) that I didn't know what to do with my current situation. One [of my children] cries all the time and my two-and-a-half-year-old wants me all the time. The speaker told me that my feelings were 'typical of a mom with two young children, and that it was important to be around others in the same stage of life.' Afterwards, several moms came up to me asked me to join a playgroup. It was exactly what I needed." Even though the kids are older now, the moms from Arlene's playgroup still get together for coffee. This sort of continuity is not at all unusual!

Lea, a working mom of two, credits the social connections provided by her mothers' group with keeping her physically well and productive. "Connecting with other moms seems to be one of the most powerful experiences that I have during the week. I find that if I miss these times, then the rest of the week is more stressful, and I need to work really hard to get the little things done."

Playgroups

Young children in playgroups are so interesting and their moms are so focused on their development that playgroups become wonderful arenas for observing and discussing human psychology. Why not, since the whole fascinating drama is unfolding right there in the sandbox? In my first child's playgroup, I entered a wonderful new realm of friendship based on being with other mothers and their children. In a way, it was like socializing in college, but with a deeper purpose created by the desire to love and nurture my children. I was drawn to a variety of mothers who all had a common goal: to be a good parent. All of these mothers had previously defined themselves through their careers, their graduate degrees, and their professional interests. We all brought our backgrounds to the playground with us, but our kids fascinated and challenged us, so our first priority was always the hot, child-oriented topic of the day. We would pass that topic back and forth in bits and snatches as we followed our children in and out of the play structures. Mothers in playgroups specialize in conducting this kind of moving conversation, and it's multitasking at its best.

We talked about parenting, relationships, nursing, weaning, sleeping strategies, routines, and playground politics. We discussed what to feed to our children, read to them, and teach them as we nursed, fed, guided, chased, and played with multiple children on the playground. We found humor in the mundane and joy in the simplicity. We shared the latest consignment store finds, since many of us had school loans to repay, were living on one income instead of two, or had a partner just starting in a career. We could also laugh at our disheveled clothes, piles of laundry, and messy houses.

One of the great things about playgroups is that, as our kids grow and change, the experience of the participating moms changes, too, following the natural progression of our kids' development. In my current sibling playgroup at our elementary school, I am having different kinds of conversations than I did in an earlier stage of parenting. No longer seeking tips on potty training (though troubleshooting is always welcome), we more seasoned moms go for other topics. Sometimes we use parenting books or women's studies books as springboards for discussions. At other times, we use our current life experiences. All of us have at least two children, and that gives us perspective and insight. Our discussions are broad ranging now: we address many topics ranging from cultural expectations and social pressures, to asserting limits and saying no, to handling the death of a parent, to setting up outreach programs at our elementary school. Playgroups are a great meeting of minds, a moms' think tank.

Work-Based Mother Support Groups

There are also many work-based support groups that you can find locally or on the Internet. Jill, a working mother of two, belongs to a support group called "WISE: Women in Science and Engineering," which is composed of postdocs and grad students. "We meet for lunch about once per week, and discuss balancing science with life. Half of us have children." Many fields where women are (or were) in the minority have excellent support groups and welcome mothers.

Support groups for working mothers abound, such as www.unlimitedmom.com. For a completely current listing, go to www.questia.com, which is one of the largest online libraries. Just search for the topic "working mother" and check out the resources available to you. For breastfeeding mothers, organizations like La Leche League International at www.lalecheleague.org offer support in a variety of venues, including face-to-face local chapter meetings.

There are also many parent and single mother support groups that can address your specific situation. For example www.troubledwith.com offers free online articles, advice, and support for working moms on topics such as life pressures, transitions, parenting children, parenting teens, abuse and addiction, love and sex. On the other hand, www.ClubMom.com and www.ivillage.com have more of a magazine style and address everything from pregnancy to Internet safety to sex to nutrition; ivillage has a hip and happening how-to tone; ClubMom feels like a village and has chat rooms on just about any topic.

Books such as *The Working Mother's Guide to Life: Strategies, Secrets, and Solutions* by Linda Mason and *The Complete Single Mother: Reassuring Answers to Your Most Challenging Concerns* by Andrea Engber and Leah Klungness are excellent toolkits filled with strategies, resources, and pointers to national support groups tailored to specific needs. Do a keyword search such as "working mother support" or "single mothers" on Google or go to www.sportofmotherhood.com for additional resources.

Self-Help/Self-Awareness Support Groups

Self-help and self-awareness groups exist in many different venues and philosophies, often with an emphasis on introspection and thoughtful self-discipline. If these groups appeal to you, use an Internet search engine like Google or watch your local papers for information. If you are searching on the Internet, try different keywords to optimize your results. You can try a general search on the keywords "meditation," "yoga," or "Tae Kwon Do," for example, or you can enter more specific keywords, such as "breathing exercises," if you already know what you want. You can even sign up for a daily meditation through www.dailyom.com. If you seek more formalized breathing and meditation techniques, go to www.artofliving.org. Alison, a working mother of two, found the breathing classes to be very helpful. She learned that "breathing in a certain manner alters your state of mind." If you struggle with self-esteem and could use a little coaching, then www.selfesteem4women.com might be the link for you.

Maybe the creative side of you feels blocked or stuck. If so, consider joining one of the writers and artist workshops that use Julia Cameron's book *The Artist's Way: A Spiritual Path to Higher Creativity*; you can join these workshops locally or online by going to www.artistsway.meetup.com.

You can also go to www.meetup.com and type in your interest and zip code in order to find others nearby who are interested in your subject matter. You then choose a face-to-face or online discussion. Signing up for classes online or at the local community college, community center, gym, or yoga studio is a great possibility.

> **MOM TIP**
>
> If you feel like you are stuck in some patterns or habits and your life feels unmanageable, you may need to look into some of the wonderful twelve-step programs available. Why not move through the baggage, face your fears, and rekindle the joy?
>
> There are twelve-step programs for people with many different issues, including those who think they (might) have a problem with alcohol, co-dependency, overeating, smoking, gambling, overspending, sex, shame, and so on. Do some research on the Internet by looking up a keyword such as "Twelve Steps" or go to "Keep Coming Back: Twelve Step Links" at www.stanice.com/links.html. Use your phone book to get local numbers. Call and ask for local meeting times.

Once you find a self-help group, try it out for a while. Give yourself enough time. Attend enough meetings to get a feeling for the group. Listen and participate. Remember, the people in the meeting are there because they are working on something, too. What do you have to lose? You are not broken; you're a person with enough awareness to want to lead a healthy and fulfilling life. If you address your shortcomings, your whole family will benefit from your efforts. It's worth a try.

Shared Challenge Support Groups

Many excellent groups address the special medical needs of parents or children. If you have need of this kind of support, hospitals, doctors, and social workers can readily point the way. You can also look online to find national organizations that support families with health issues, such as breast cancer or autism. Almost all of these organizations will have local chapters. Newspapers, city guides, and local parenting magazines are also great resources. Of course, online discussion groups provide convenience and anonymity and can even center on topics such as raising challenging children. For more about grief support groups, go to Chapter 8: Being Hit by a Truck, or visit www.sportofmotherhood.com.

B. Building New Groups

If you can't find the group that you need, you can create one. Start by placing an ad in local publications or by putting up flyers in libraries, local coffee shops or small grocery stores, bookstores, the YMCA, or on school bulletin boards. Make sure your ad or flyer is clear about the group's purpose, and direct interested people to contact you. If you're using flyers, don't put too many up; gauge the response first so that you aren't swamped. When starting a group, keep in mind that it takes time to grow. Begin small and add people gradually. If it becomes necessary to limit numbers, put a ceiling on members and encourage latecomers to start a second group. If this happens, you've hit on a hot topic.

A mother at our school wanted to start a parent education group tailored to mothers of elementary and middle-school kids. After she asked around a bit and found some interest, she opted to write a blurb and submit it to the school newsletter. Here it is, rewritten as a template you can adapt to your own use:

Advertisement for Starting a Mothers' Group with a Specific Focus

What: A mothers' group committed to support all of the relationships that are experienced by women, e.g., wife, mother, sibling and child. Many moms may find it difficult to balance the conflicting demands of the various roles. Come and meet other women who share the same challenges and the same desires to work toward having more harmony in their lives.

How: During the first part of the meeting, all members will check in. This allows everyone to share any issue or concern. The next part is a participatory discussion on a chosen topic. At the end of the first meeting, members will select the future topics, set meeting dates and times. Reading materials may be suggested. Guest speakers may be invited to join and participate in a session.

When: The first meeting will be on Wednesday, 10/13, at 8:45 a.m. to 10:00 a.m., at _____. Please be willing to participate and share ideas and experiences. Group limited to ten participants.

If interested, please contact _____.

Build Shared Interest Groups: A Case Study of Growing a Village

Another way to build support is by forming a group through an already existing network. A school, church, or mothers' group is a great place to begin, since people in these networks are much more likely to be available. Something great happened at Fairmeadow, my children's elementary school. A school-wide outreach program grew from the successes of an informal Mom's Night Out program, which Mary Kraemer and I had begun the year before. The outreach program simply tapped into the already existing energy, interests, and enthusiasm of the school community.

As the program evolved, people came to us with even more ideas and began starting some of their own events. Soon we had restaurant, crafting, basket weaving, and movie nights. We also had picnics, after-school craft parties for the kids, and weekly sibling playgroups. By the end of the year, our PTA President Hazel Watson wanted us to be more inclusive, since dads and kids were now getting involved.

Over that summer, we launched the Fairmeadow United Network. The program now includes: Moms', Dads', and Parents' Socials that involve game nights, rock climbing, craft nights, scrapbooking workshops, softball games and so forth; a Babysitting Co-op; Weekly Sibling and All-Age Playgroups; informal after-school sports led by parents; walking, hiking, and running buddies for adults and kids; a Parent Ed/Support Group for Moms of Elementary Age Kids; Book Groups; Meals on Wheels; Birth Announcements.

There's more! Events for dads and kids, like playing Laserquest and going to see a baseball game, are also on the calendar. We have Red Cross CPR and First Aid classes for both parents and teachers. It appears that a mom-and-child book club is also on the way. After two successful years, the Mom's Night Out Program was voted onto the PTA board. A year later, the Fairmeadow United Network obtained an operating budget to cover some supply and snack costs. The program is open to the whole school, not just PTA members and their families.

We are growing a village at our school with the help of all the people who set up and enjoy our network activities. By providing the F.U.N. infrastructure, we have created a way to focus the various needs and interests of our particular school and bring in new people and new leaders. The network, which includes contacts and point people, creates an organized way to handle the incoming information, streamline events and advertising, and gain permission for varied events without burdening the principal and PTA president.

People can access the current information and contacts through the school paper, the school e-news, the PTA meeting minutes, designated advertising space, and the back of the school directory. We are always open to new ideas and have gotten so many ideas from our lively and engaged community that we will have to spread them out over the next few years.

To better serve our particular community's needs, we cast a wide net. Being mindful of the time constraints of both working and nonworking parents, we schedule events for days, nights, weekdays and weekends. We learn what works and what we can improve for the next time. Our school's rich cultural diversity also factors into our planning.

We dovetail events whenever we can. Here are three examples:

1. We used the All-Age Summer Playgroup as a meeting place for creating the F.U.N. infrastructure since the playgroup was already happening; kids could play while parents brainstormed and streamlined our information.
2. By selling "gently used" clothes for $1 per item at our fall fair, we created a sense of the school community as an extended family passing clothes along. We raised some additional funds for the playgroup and from the profits we treated moms and kids to some hot chocolate once a month at the All-Age Playgroup.
3. We used some of our craft nights to make decorations, such as tissue flowers, flags, and origami boats, for the annual school fundraiser.

Our overarching goal: to provide fun opportunities for people to socialize and build community.

Below is a brief history of F.U.N. at Fairmeadow Elementary.

F.U.N. = Fairmeadow United Network. F.U.N.'s mission: community building. It's a supplementary program that does not drain or strain the current volunteer pool. In 2005/2006, F.U.N. had another successful year with new growth.

- F.U.N.'s Annual Goals for
    - **Year 1** (2002–2003) Originally called "MNO" or Moms Night Out. Goal: to connect moms.
    - **Year 2** (2003–2004) Goal: to connect moms, dads, and Fairmeadow siblings and to vary activities to address school's diverse interests and cultures. Meals on Wheels and Clothing Exchange began informally. Summer playgroup started. Emphasis on bringing in kindergarten families.
    - **Year 3** (2004–2005) Voted on and named F.U.N. or Fairmeadow United Network. Goal: to bring in dads and kids even more, to address working parent needs by rotating times and days of events, Wheels on Meals and Babysitting Co-op officially added. Moms' Parent Ed Group + Book Club started. After-School All-Age Playgroup and pick-up sports added. Moms vs. Kids Softball Game at End of School-year BBQ added.

- o **Year 4** (2005–2006) Goal: to bridge schools and offer more "in-reach." Emphasis on giving Bus Kids something to take home on All-Age Playgroup Days. Parent Co-ed Softball Game + BBQ added (Fairmeadow vs. another school).
- o **Year 5** (2006–2007) Goal: to provide free or low-cost family events (as distinct from Just Sign Ups) and participate in community outreach project with Youth Community Service (YCS).
- Calendar for next 2006–07 year (Thanks to Brainstorming Meeting + Community Input):
    - o September — Family Board Game Night
    - o October — Family Community Outreach Project with Youth Community Service
    - o November — Moms Dinner Out
    - o December — free
    - o January — Family Hike in Huddart Park
    - o February — Dads and Kids Laserquest
    - o March — Auction Decorations and Craft Night (Moms and Kids)
    - o April — Parent Co-ed Softball Game vs. other schools + BBQ afterwards
    - o May — Family Campout @ Fairmeadow! (Or until 10:30 p.m.)
    - o June — Family Baseball game at Stanford

Our village continues to grow.

Some Ideas for Growing Your Own Village:

I. Begin a Shared Interest Group

1. **Start Small.** Think of your first year as a pilot year. You will be trying things out to see what works and what doesn't work for your particular community. Begin with one or two programs and build from there. Some easy places to start: playgroups, Mom's Night

Out, craft and scrapbook nights. Also see if you can get a buddy to set this up with you.

- **Playgroups.** Create a weekly playgroup with moms who drop off kids at school and have younger children. Arrange to meet right after school drop-off at a nearby park. You can also set up an after-school, all-age playgroup. Even if parents and kids can only hang out for thirty minutes to one hour, the playgroup builds community. During the summer, you can arrange a weekly all-age playgroup to keep people connected and allow incoming kindergarteners and parents a chance to get to know each other before school begins.

- **Mom's Night Out.** Gather ideas and areas of interest. Pick a fun restaurant for the first night out. Ask if you can use the school library or multipurpose room for other things like a craft/scrapbook night, a workshop, or a movie. Ask everyone to bring a snack or beverage to share. Some moms will have to cancel at the last minute as things do come up. Expect it. No problem. These evenings are meant to be guilt-free for everyone.

- **Frequency.** Set up one event at a time and enjoy it. Set up the next event for a month or two later. See how it goes. Remember that you are building something, and that takes time. Don't overcommit yourself or others.

2. **Broaden Ownership and Interest.** Consider meeting at different houses for your meetings. That often helps people get to know each other and feel part of the community you are creating. Keep the atmosphere relaxed and low-key. Offer opportunities for people to volunteer at different levels: hosting a meeting, suggesting a book, bringing questions to start a discussion.

3. **Get the Word Out.** Experiment to find out what works in your community. Some favorite places to publicize events for parents are flyers, posters, and school newspaper and e-news or leaflets. Include basic information about the group, along with contact names, phone numbers, and email addresses. Use playful wording to send out a welcoming signal. Talk about moms recharging their batteries, giving themselves a boost or the opportunity to get more

than a five-minute chat with some fellow school parents. If you are centered at a school, ask the principal if you can put your event on a school announcement board. Ask each of your members to try to bring one to two people to your next event.

4. **Manage Your Expectations.** Sometimes you will have a few people and sometimes a lot more. Relax and enjoy whatever turnout you have. Go with the flow. Small and large groups each have their benefits.

5. **Be Consistent.** If you are the main contact, always have a backup (or two) who can stand in for you if you can't make the meeting. Groups thrive on consistency, and one lackluster meeting can knock the group off track. The more frequently the group meets, the more likely it is that the group leader will have to miss a meeting, so be prepared. Pass a "kit" or supplies on if you need to. (For a description of a kit, see Grow an Outreach Group, item #13.)

II. Grow an Outreach Group

1. **Grow the Program.** Once your interest group is rolling along, you can begin to expand it. If you want, you can alternate dinner night months with craft/scrapbook nights hosted in the school multipurpose room or school library. Bring some goodies and drinks, then rotate snacks or ask everyone to bring a snack or beverage to share. Different types of events will probably attract different people. Some find it easier to have something to do as they visit or get to know people while others can't stand crafts and prefer a night on the town.

2. **Co-lead.** It is fun to develop a program with someone. You energize each other, can problem-solve, and lighten the load through the teamwork.

3. **Vary Events as the Program Grows.** As the program gathers energy and participation, you can vary the events more.

4. **Draw on Your Community Talent Pool.** Ask around for talents in your community or add a column to a sign-up sheet asking those in the community if they have a talent that they might like to share. Would anyone be willing to host a workshop either for free or at cost of materials?

5. **Gather Data.** What are areas of shared interest in your particular community? Post a notice with some ideas and blanks for suggestions, have a poster and sign-up sheets at Back to School Night. You can use categories like Moms', Dads', and Parents' Nights Out, Exercise Groups, Book Clubs, Playgroups, General Volunteer, Other Interests, and Suggestions. Ask people to provide their names, phone numbers, and email addresses and indicate their interests. Put something on the table to draw attention: a fun guessing game, a raffle, or an election for a group acronym.

6. **Brainstorm to Build the Program.** Brainstorm with as many people as you can. Get all the ideas down, remembering that you will edit later. Provide members of the community with a variety of ways to give their input. Send out emails and ask people to forward to others who might be interested. Dovetail with already existing community events and gather information from them. Email chains also keep people in the loop.

7. **Build your Base.** Get contacts or point people for each program. Put question marks next to possible contacts and write "confirmed" when they sign on. Build on already existing interest and energy. Diversify base and draw from different social or cultural groups. Remind contacts that they are moms or dads first. If something becomes a burden, let the point people know. The outreach program is not meant to drain the volunteer pool or reserves, rather to add energy and connection. Get the word out any way that you can: flyers, existing newsletters, email.

8. **Community Name and Involvement.** Get the group or school to vote on its name or acronym. List the potential names on a poster or blackboard. People can put a penny or marker down on their favorite name or add a new one to the list.

9. **Stand Out.** You can brand your group. Have a fun logo, catchy name or signature color to alert people to your events and news.

10. **Create a Template.** As the program grows, put together an easy-to-read handout with contact information and frequency of events. See Appendix A for the Fairmeadow United Network Template. It goes in the Back-to-School packets at the end of summer and is printed in the school directory. Extra copies are kept in the school

office. The F.U.N. Calendar of Events in the school newspaper includes the following categories: Monthly Events, By Arrangement, and Weekly.

11. **Delegate.** Think of sensible, productive ways to share the work. If you are publicizing events in a school or church newsletter, for example, see if someone in your group will take charge of collecting and submitting updates to the editor. This subeditor can also send reminders to all contacts about the upcoming newspaper submission deadlines. You can have a webmaster to manage the Family Web Page and volunteers who update the Family Outreach Bulletin Board.

12. **Get Free Events.** Ask organizations if they would be willing to cut you a deal for a group of moms or parents in return for some publicity.

13. **Kits.** Put together a kit for both the older and younger set to amp up a group. A playgroup kit can be created from donations or small funds and can include some of the following: bubbles, chalk, jump rope, balls, Frisbees, and beads w/pipe cleaners. A kit for older kids can include a bead set with hemp, pop-up tent with tunnel, a plastic tarp, stomp rockets, a face painting kit, deck of cards, travel board games and a bag of superballs. Bubbles and chalk are relatively inexpensive and can be used up and replaced easily.

14. **Understand the Launch Window.** Keep in mind that it takes a bit of extra effort and energy to begin or grow a program during the initial launch period. You are checking in with contacts and making sure that they know what to do, where to be, and how to get word of new developments out to the community. You'll also want to know how they are feeling about their commitments. Some programs might not sustain interest. Cut programs that don't catch on so that you can move on to those that do. You can also create seasonal options.

Wrap-up

One thing I have learned is that **support goes both ways**. As you watch others grow and cheer them on towards their goals, you will find the strength and courage to take another step towards your own goals. While writing *The Sport of Motherhood*, I emailed some friends: "I have new wings, but I need to BELIEVE in order to fly." My cheerleaders and encouragers helped me to overcome discouraging hurdles and take my next steps. So will yours.

MOM TIP

The bottom line is: get connected and get support so that you succeed.

If you want to work more on identifying accountability buddies and goal progress, go to the exercises below. With your support network forming up outside the home, and teamwork turned on inside your home, you are ready to start training. Let's move on to Chapter 5: Mom Training Tips and Tools.

EXERCISES

Take a step toward creating a network by listening to others. Encourage and support someone, and then ask someone for support. Compare life maps and goals. Give the exercises below some of your time. Take a moment to think about what progress means to you.

Warm Up: Reflective Stretches

List two goals that you have set for yourself in the past. Put a checkmark next to the ones you kept.

1. _____
2. _____

List one obstacle that you encountered for each one.

1. _____
2. _____

List two new goals that you would like to work toward this year. Circle your first choice.

1. _____
2. _____

Practice: New Skills

Assess your Support Network

Use the chart below to assess the strength of your support network. Are there enough people in your network? Are they in the best roles for them? Can you count on them?

1. **Accountability Buddy**: Does she/he hold you or help you to be accountable to goals of your choice? Often accountability involves just showing up!
2. **Cheerleader**: Does she/he encourage or support your goals? If someone believes in you, she/he can help you to take risks and grow.
3. **Mentor**: Is she/he a mentor at times or in certain areas of your life?

Support Network Assessment Table

	Name	Name	Name	Name
Accountability Buddy				
Cheerleader				
Mentor				

Creating New Support Networks

1. Do you want to start a group around a hobby or interest?
2. If so, what kind of format or setting would you prefer?
3. List three ways to get the word out in your community.

    a. _____

    b. _____

    c. _____

Cool Down

Write down one person that you can ask to be a mentor or accountability buddy for your goal, or write down one group, class, or chat room you can join that will provide a possible mentor or accountability buddy.

_____

CHAPTER 5

Mom Training Tips and Tools

> ▶ R U having trouble getting started with any goal?
> ▶ Do U have trouble saying "NO"?
> ▶ How about identifying pressure points N your week + better preparing 4 them?

For mothers, pacing is one of the greatest challenges. Sometimes it seems like kids are little scientists running chaos experiments. And their timing can be uncanny:

> Somehow, ten minutes before time to leave, things happened. Murphy's law, except that it was the norm in my house on school mornings. Someone had to go potty or the baby spit up all over me, all over herself—you name it. After the tenth time of reminding my second child to put on her socks (she couldn't find any comfortable socks that stayed up on her ankles), I would take a deep breath and head towards the baby jogger.
>
> Time to get moving or we would really have to hustle. After loading the five-month-old, I would look for the two-year-old and often have to chase her down. She liked to play hide and seek. Sometimes I would turn around and she would have stripped naked—right when we were supposed to be heading out the door to calmly walk to our elementary school.

Just as runners pace themselves differently for a 5K or a half-marathon, for a hill or a flat course, moms need to train differently for different phases of their lives. A runner does not run full sprint at the beginning of a longer race, and a mother who has toddlers or preschoolers needs to build in extra time for potty breaks, lost socks, tantrums, and other mishaps. An all-out sprint to school with no time to spare invites trouble. As you begin training to meet your goals, you will still be navigating through a mom's day, and that means potential distractions right, left, and center. Once you are in training, you can handle the distractions without losing your stride.

The first step of training is: get started doing what you have ALREADY planned. That means finding the time you need, allowing for trial and error, assessing your strategies, logging progress, and handling schedule conflicts. In this chapter, we will go over how to implement your personalized **Strategic Plan**. You have your goal; now we are going to focus on Getting There. We will also go over what to do if you cannot get started or get stuck. This is where the action takes place. Let's get going!

One Step at a Time: Your Implementation Plans

In order to take action, you have to know what steps to take to reach your goal. If you make the steps too small, you'll be tempted to combine multiple steps or skip them. If you make a step too large, you may never take it because it's intimidating or you can't find the time. The key to success is plotting out realistic steps for you in your current situation. There is a certain satisfaction to crossing a step off your list, so try to find the right "size" for your steps. Remember learning how to estimate back in Kindergarten and first grade? Estimate how many peanuts are in the jar. If you eat two peanuts an hour, estimate how long it will take you to eat 255 peanuts. Here's another chance to practice that great skill, with a twist. You have a goal and a plan: as you implement your plan, you'll be focusing on your goal and estimating how to get there.

Let's go back to Alexis and work through her first priority to get a better idea of how to create a detailed Implementation plan. First, Alexis wrote down the information from her Overview Plan, leaving space to fill out Getting There, Obstacles, and Resources:

> **First Objective:** Improve marital relations
>
> **Strategy:** Let Will know how much I love him

Goal: Make Will more of a priority

Current Status: We're so busy and I forget. Will isn't very verbal, so I just don't bother.

Obstacles:

1. Not doing it because he doesn't; no time
2. Feel exhausted and covered with kids when he comes home from work
3. Hard to switch gears and relate to anyone who is over three-feet tall

Resources: Hallmark store, email, and friends for ideas (date nights and how to switch gears)

Allies: Mom, Dad, friends

Steps:

1. Get some cards.
2. Send an "I love you" email to Will.
3. Ask around for some fun date night ideas.
4. Get off the computer or phone or television when he gets home and give him my attention.
5. Take a shower and wash off the day at end of day so that I can put aside my mom hat and put on my adult/woman/spouse hat.
6. Set up date night for once a week or every other week. Can get a sitter or have date night at home after kids go to bed (set table up with nice dinner or take-out, rent a movie, play a board game).
7. Reassess after one month.

Pay-Off: Better marriage, happier at home.

Alexis spent some time thinking about the problem and possible solutions. Most of the needed changes had to do with transitions, especially the transition time when her husband came home from work. She decided to put things down, get off the phone, or pause the kids' television program when he came through the door and give him ten minutes of her time. Then she could go back to whatever she and the kids were doing.

After the kids were in bed, she could also take a quick shower to wash off the kid day and switch gears and get into adult mode.

She also wanted to tell her husband at least once a day that she loved him. She could say it, write a card or email, or call him on the phone. She could even leave the cards or notes in his sock drawer, taped to the bureau, or in his briefcase.

For the first couple of days, Will did not know what to think. Everyone was excited to see him when he came home from a long day at the office. They got off the phone and television. He got to hear about their day. This really brightened his mood and set a nice tone for the evening. Now he wanted to help his wife more with dinner, dishes, and bedtime routines.

> **MOM TIP**
>
> After the kids were in bed, Alexis was also making a real effort to hang out with him and visit. She seemed to be interested in him again. Not that she wasn't interested before—it was just that she had become so distracted by the kids.

He began to look forward to the nightly discussions and weekly date nights. After a few weeks, he began to feel lucky again. His wife loved him. He had great kids. . . . Home began to feel more like a home. The two of them now counted on the fun hang-out time after the kids were in bed, and he had more in common again with the woman he married. The notes and cards from her prompted him to begin saying "I love you" more often to her. Fairy tale? Possibly. Fairy tales do come true, but not unless you try!

Can't Get Started? Take Smaller Steps

If your goal feels too big, break it down into smaller steps. If you feel overwhelmed just thinking about the journey or goal, focus on taking the first step. You can begin—one step at a time.

Mom Tip

Try not to make two major changes to your life at once. "If you want to BOTH exercise more and start painting, choose which one comes first." —Tara

Trying to start two changes at once doubles the likelihood of failure. Create the Implementation Plan for your first goal, keeping these things in mind.

Tess uses a favorite mantra: "One step at a time." This also applies to "Don't worry about what you can't change." She says the "mantra slices through pointless worry/frustration and makes you focus on action that you can take to bring about change." Once you are into the "doing" mode rather than the "worry" mode, you feel a lot better.

Honor Thy Personal Time

The very existence of my book, *The Sport of Motherhood*, attests to the practical value of this advice. After realizing how important doing art was to me, I created the space for my art. I took Julia Cameron's lead in her book *The Artist's Way: A Spiritual Path to Higher Creativity* and put art dates on my calendar, using the time for drawing and writing. From Cameron, I learned to protect that time and honor my art commitment to myself. I learned to say no to some new commitments and even some social outings and yes to myself. Through her writing exer-

Mom Story

When clarifying objectives, "the first question I ask is whether the goal is attainable from where I am now. It may be that I need to achieve other things that are goals in their own right before I can tackle that one. For example, if the goal is to be an accomplished painter, but I have never painted before, then the goal of learning how to paint needs to be dealt with first. I may find that having learned to paint, I no longer have the goal of being really good, since I may have moved in a different direction in that time. The strategy is simply to break a problem into segments, and get started. If I wait until I have more time, that never happens" (Tess). One step at a time brings progress.

cises and journaling I also learned to get messy again and not worry about the outcome.

As I eliminated old expectations, creating new awareness, I unblocked my creative spirit. I could let the process unfold. I let myself do the bad art to get to the good art. In order to even do the bad art, I had to just make the time to do it by beginning with baby steps. I could do a little bit each week. Slowly, the focus moved from visual arts to the written word.

My art dates expanded to a daily minimum of writing hours as I fervently wrote what was to become a memoir. I would sit down at 9 o'clock every night after the kids were in bed and write until midnight or so. My creative time didn't interfere with the kids' lives and my husband Keen and I would make sure to get our time. Ironically, I felt like I had even more energy as my identity evolved and expanded. I could then transfer this positive energy back onto my family. Connected to my pre-kid self and stimulated, I felt integrated and whole.

There are some mom-traps that can make it doubly hard to keep some of your time for yourself. Oddly, being distracted can start to feel good. After all, it means that someone needs you, and it feels good to be needed. Then, most moms are athletes when it comes to troubleshooting forty things at once, and athletes like to use their skills! Something in your reflexes starts shouting, "Bring it on, I'm ready for it." When this happens, it can be hard to pull yourself away from all of the action and be with yourself, for yourself. Do it, even if it's only meditating or gardening for ten minutes. You'll return to your family a stronger, more positive person.

Use Your Calendar as a Tool

Getting your commitment on a calendar can help out. Audrey uses her date book: "I like to schedule things because that is how I get stuff done. For art: I know that I have certain exhibits. For exercise, I find that I need to set up exercise appointments to lock me in and move me forward. For reading, I probably wouldn't be reading as much if I did not have book clubs."

Devote a bit of time each week to working towards your goal. Put it on the calendar and honor your "date" as you would any other scheduled commitment. Work with your partner or a friend or hire a sitter to care for the kids. Write your personal time down on a calendar: 2–3 p.m. reading time,

8–10 a.m. Saturday sketch at the Bay lands, 7–8 a.m. Curves [Fitness Center]. Honor your commitment to yourself and keep your date. Fill up.

Mom Tip

Keep in mind that many "goals" may just be about ways of living. You are trying to develop new "habits" and new routines. Success is about taking action, enjoying the process, and letting go of the results. Remember that it takes time to develop new habits. Give yourself the time needed to succeed before abandoning a goal.

Make Feel-Good Lists

Pat, a working mom of two, finds active organization enables her to design her life: "In general, I am a HUGE believer in having a 'balanced' lifestyle. Everything should be done in moderation. I like to enjoy life, so all the free time I have is devoted to doing so. But I get satisfaction from doing things that others would consider a much larger chore than I do. For example, I am extremely organized, and that allows me to do as much as I do. If I wasn't as organized, I wouldn't get half as much done. I have ongoing task lists, etc."

Now that you have a plan, you have to make TIME to live your plan. To do that, you have to look at your current life and figure out how to carve out the time. Because moms are so busy, that means that you'll probably have to cull some activities or habits that eat up time. The only way to figure out what you can drop from your day is to figure out what your life priorities are.

Making Time

If you don't have time for starting your new goals, then you have to make it. You can't make time for everything or please everyone. Once you identify your primary objectives, you can prioritize your day and your week.

1. Create a 24-hour grid in your notebook using a ruler or by creating a table in your computer file. Write down your schedule over the course of a week. Feel free to add to the following suggested categories: Sleep, Exercise, Kid Prep, Shower/Dress, Meal Prep,

Meals, School Prep or Work, Travel Time (if applicable), Kid Activities, Housework, School Volunteer, Meeting and Mothers' Group. If it helps to schedule in a bit of Personal Time, do so. See 24-Hour Time Use Grid example below.

2. Using a highlighter or a pencil, block out any mandatory items.
3. Also be sure to block out required sleep needs.
4. Then look at the optional activities. Do you see ways to combine activities or responsibilities so that you can streamline your energy as well as create a bit of free time? Are there low-priority items that are taking up too much time?
5. Play around with any optional items and see if you can find the time you need to start your new objective.

24-Hour Time Use Grid (Example)

	Sunday	Monday	Tuesday	Wednesday	Thursday	Friday	Saturday
12 – 6 A.M.	Sleep	Sleep	Sleep	Sleep	Sleep	Sleep	Sleep
6 – 7 A.M.	Sleep	Personal Time	Exercise	Personal Time	Exercise	Shower/Dress	Exercise
7 – 8 A.M.	Sleep	Kid Prep	Kid Prep	Kid Prep	Kid Prep	Kid Prep	Exercise
8 – 9 A.M.	Kid Prep		Housework	Exercise/Shower	Housework	School Volunteer	
9 – 10 A.M.	Church	Work or School Prep	Shower/Dress	Work or School Prep	Housework	School Volunteer	
10 – 11 A.M.	Church	Work or School Prep	Mothers' Group	Work or School Prep	Shower/Dress		Kid Activities
11 A.M. – 12 P.M.	Church/Meal Prep	Work or School Prep	Mothers' Group	Work or School Prep	Grocery Store	Kid Activity	Kid Activities
12 – 1 P.M.	Meal	Work or School Prep		Work or School Prep	Grocery Store		Meal Prep and Meal
1 – 2 P.M.	Family Time		Housework	Housework		Housework	Family Time
2 – 3 P.M.	Family Time						Family Time
3 – 4 P.M.	Family Time	Kid Activities	Kid Activities	Kid Activities	Kid Activities	Kid Activities	Family Time
4 – 5 P.M.	Family Time	Kid Activities	Kid Activities	Kid Activities	Kid Activities	Kid Activities	Family Time
5 – 6 P.M.	Meal Prep	Meal Prep	Meal Prep	Meal Prep	Meal Prep	Meal Prep	Family Time

(continued)

24-Hour Time Use Grid (Example continued)

	Sunday	Monday	Tuesday	Wednesday	Thursday	Friday	Saturday
6 - 7 P.M.	Meal	Meeting	Meal	Meal	Meal	Meal	Meal
7 - 8 P.M.	Kid Prep	Meeting	Kid Prep	Kid Prep	Kid Prep	Kid Prep	Kid Prep
8 - 9 P.M.	Kid Prep	Meeting	Kid Prep	Kid Prep	Kid Prep	Kid Prep	Kid Prep
9 - 10 P.M.							
10 - 11 P.M.	Sleep	Sleep	Sleep	Sleep	Sleep		
11 P.M - 12 A.M	Sleep	Sleep	Sleep	Sleep	Sleep	Sleep	Sleep

Sonia, a stay-at-home mother who home-schools her three children, lives in a more rural area of the country. It takes quite a bit of time to go to town, to visit a friend, to run an errand. By being a little organized with her children's schedules, she can get the most out of her travel time. "I organize my life with a calendar and by combining as many trips into one as possible. For example, we try to have friends for each child from the same geographic area on the same day. Or if we have a class near the child's friend, we try to arrange get-togethers around that time. I also try to couple one child's activity with special alone time with my other children."

Perhaps you can edit your commitments to create space for some free time, down time, or thinking time. If you carve out some blank time on your calendar, you can allow things to bubble up. Who are you? What excites you? Don't immediately fill the time. Let yourself enjoy it. Give yourself time to be still. Who knows what desires and interests—read potential new and exciting priorities—may emerge if you allow yourself time to tune into your mind. The next task is to figure out where you can fit in the time for the steps to your goals.

How Much Time Is Enough?

Only you can answer this question. Just what is a realistic weekly minimum goal? Don't be afraid to experiment. Try to figure out just how much time each of your steps is going to take and what the time frame is for completing them. This can help you to figure out how much time to allow. You also need to consider your own energy levels at different times of the day.

Are you an early bird or a night owl? Choose time when you'll be most able to accomplish your steps.

> **MOM TIP**
>
> If you cannot think of where to begin, then start with one hour a week of goal time.

Listen to books on tape while driving or walking. Read goal-related materials while on the bus, subway, or Stairmaster, or while waiting for your kids at school. Arrive twenty minutes early for carpool or pickup so that you have some thinking time in your car. Set your alarm to wake up thirty minutes earlier, several days a week. There is your hour. You can do this.

> **MOM TIP**
>
> Here's another strategy. Tess thinks "in terms of events rather than time. For example, the goal might be attending a minimum number of events (perhaps getting to the free jazz concerts at least once in the summer). Aim for that, and more is a bonus. It applies to exercise, creative stuff, etc. I find the hard part is getting started, rather than total time spent. Just using the event itself as a measure of progress gets me going."

You will feel more inspired to complete a task if you believe that you can do it. If you don't believe in yourself, no one else will. When you get a small victory, you feel better about yourself and have a brighter outlook. If your objective feels unattainable, you will get discouraged and be less likely to do the footwork. If you need others to help you set realistic goals, find them! This is where support networks and accountability buddies play a pivotal role.

Elise, a tech sales professional and mom of one, offers this advice: "If a goal seems unattainable, I simply start. I always have minimums. At work I had it for the ugly tasks like cold-calling, and presently I have it for my exercise program."

> **Mom Story**
>
> Annie applies a reward system to motivate her to do items on her to-do list that she does not enjoy but needs to do. "I hate to iron. But I hate even more to take shirts into a laundry and pay to have someone iron them. So, when I have to iron a mound of shirts, I 'pay' myself $1/shirt, and that money goes into a little bank and is saved up for a Disneyland trip (last time, I had over $100!). I call it the Laundry Fairy fund; any/all money that comes out of pockets in the laundry also goes into this fund." She builds in a reward system that moves her to take action and benefits the whole family. Your reward system can also be just for you—but you get the idea.

Keep this in mind: you want realistic minimum goals so that you are successful and will keep working towards your over-arching goals. Anything more is a BONUS. If you feel like you are meeting your weekly goals, you will feel better about yourself and in turn find more energy.

Taking on New Commitments

The world doesn't stop just because you are starting something new. You are still going to have people clambering for your time. How do you handle new commitments when you just finished making time for yourself? When you consider a time commitment, think about how that commitment affects your family and your goals. Even if you feel like you are letting someone down, only you can accurately assess your energy level and enthusiasm. It's better to politely say no to someone than to overextend yourself.

When you are running on fumes, you are more likely to be slogging through the day rather than enjoying the journey or sights. Figure out how to avoid draining your energy reserves with an additional responsibility unless it fits in with your goals.

Some say that 90 percent of life is just showing up. I do believe that showing up means a lot; however, showing up for a social outing versus hosting one are two different animals. You know the behind-the-scenes work involved in running the show. Don't listen to, "It's no big deal." Many projects and volunteer activities are appealing. Resist that appeal while you assess whether or not your participation makes sense to you. Go through your checklist when you consider a new responsibility or commitment using **EFFECT**:

1. **EVALUATE** the commitment. How much time is involved? Ask to get more details if necessary.
2. Assess whether it **FITS** in your current Strategic Plan. If this commitment is outside the scope, perhaps you need to toss it. If it fits, continue.
3. Assess whether it **FITS** with your abilities. Everyone has different talents. If someone is asking you to do something that you are REALLY BAD at doing, it will probably take up even more time than you thought. If so, toss it, unless this is something you WANT to learn how to do.
4. Where can you **EDIT** your current to-do list? If you already have a full plate, adding one commitment means taking another one off.
5. **CONFESS** to yourself why you are considering this commitment. For yourself or for others? Any people-pleasing involved? If guilt is the only reason, perhaps you should let this one pass.
6. What is the current **TONE** in your home? Is anyone sick or going through a difficult phase? Has a recent crisis left you drained, needing some time to refuel?

If the new commitment does not meet your **EFFECT** criteria, then say no. You may say it politely:

- No thank you.
- This commitment doesn't work for me right now.
- I have enough commitments.
- I already have a full plate.

Write down your own phrases using the word no. Say them aloud. Practice them with a friend or partner. (This is also addressed in the end-of-chapter exercises.)

Consider coming up with some funny ones. Humor can lighten the situation and lessen the blow of your refusal. How about:

- I'd love to help, but my schedule is tighter than a pair of pre-kid jeans.
- That sounds like a worthwhile cause, but my spare time bank is empty.
- I know that you really need help, but the laundry (or dinner or cleaning) fairy is on vacation.
- If you find a way to clone me, I'd be happy to help.

If you want some time to think a decision over, apply the 24-hour strategy: "Thank you. Could I think it over for 24 hours and get back to you?" If they say yes, sit with the possibility and see how it feels. This gives you time to get used to the idea, do more research if you need to, or check in with a spouse, friend, or accountability buddy for a reality check.

Pretend you are taking on the new responsibility. Are you still excited and enthusiastic, or are you anxious and short-tempered after 24 hours? If the latter, just say "no" to the commitment. If the former, run through your EFFECT list again and ask yourself if the commitment will ADD energy or DRAIN your energy. Then make your decision and enjoy it! Don't look back and second-guess yourself. You will have other opportunities come your way, and you can make decisions based on new information then.

Sometimes you need to evaluate whether you can continue with a commitment. Sometimes the EFFECT changes. You already have the commitment, but something unexpected has come up, or the balance of time in you life has simply changed. Which is more important: appearing to be reliable, or being sane? We have to juggle the many variables of motherhood. It's

> **Mom Story**
>
> Gina, a mother of one who works from home as a tax consultant and writer, says, "I learned how to say 'no' when I became a mom. I resigned from several non-profit boards, I say no to friends sometimes and I say no to my husband (who might try to schedule a 'fun' dinner party on a Saturday night during my busy season). I keep the baby's schedule as the top priority. If she is well rested, she is happy, and that makes life much easier for us."

okay to exit a commitment, just try to give the friend or group that you are helping time to absorb your departure.

On the flip side, sometimes a commitment tries to outgrow its initial EFFECT. For example, the organizer of a big project, like a walkathon, will sometimes try to tap volunteers for additional meetings or tasks. Why now—you're already on hand. Be prepared to explain that you have already committed for what you can do. Hold the line at what works for you!

The same thing goes for controlling kids' schedules. Some people like to have only one activity per child, while others say one sport or activity plus one instrument or language. If your have several children, even one activity per child may feel like too much. If so, where can you edit? Maybe accept fewer social commitments on the weekends.

> **MOM TIP**
>
> Some families choose to have either Saturday or Sunday as family days. They even turn down birthday party invitations and do not schedule play dates for the designated "off-day." Since the weeks are busy, these families create the white space on their calendar and protect the downtime or hang-out time for their own families.

Implementing Your Plans

Getting started can be the hardest part. It is so easy to put your goal training off one more week or month. If you wait until the stars are aligned just right, you may never get started and give up before you have begun. Just take the first small step. Give yourself three weeks, three meetings, or three classes and then see how you feel. Come on, you can do almost anything for three weeks.

If you are trying something really different, the first few steps can feel awkward, and you may feel as if you are in someone else's shoes. Keep it simple and keep going. You can find your stride.

Minimum/Bonus Strategy

Record the time you put towards your goal each week. Note the patterns over several weeks. Compare the hours for each week and determine the average hours. Does the average feel like too much of a stretch? If so, make your minimum below those hours. Take one week at a time. If you put a bit of time into each week, you are SUCCESSFUL. Any more time is a bonus. Just as a child learns to sit up before he or she crawls, stands before walking, and walks before running, each little step you take towards your goal is progress. Don't be impatient with yourself. You can gradually add more time if you choose.

Adapt to your needs and abilities. Jackie wanted to add yoga to her life after the birth of her second child. She found *Itsy Bitsy Yoga: Poses to Help Your Baby Sleep Longer, Digest Better, and Grow Stronger* by Helen Garabedian and *Baby Om: Yoga for Mothers and Babies* by Laura Staton and Sarah Perron. The latter book "helped me do yoga at home because my problem was getting to class."

Jackie began mom/baby yoga when her son was six weeks old. Not only did she enjoy the yoga, but her son also did. He "loves it when I move his legs. He knows his arms will go next. He loves the sequence." The books taught her how to hold the baby while doing yoga and how to incorporate him into the poses. "You hold the baby certain ways so he balances you." Each pose offers "a way to connect with the baby."

Trial and Error

After three or so weeks, you may say "Forget this!" or "What was I thinking?" The new schedule or class does not work for you. Okay then, time to reconsider. Consider this your grand experiment. You are a scientist trying to find a cure or an artist painting a new picture; find the analogy that makes trial and error okay, even fun. Try another approach or angle. If you notice that you look forward to your goal date time, then you are on the right track.

Maybe you need to change gears altogether and work towards a different goal for now. You have gained information and insight just by taking those first few steps. So now you can make a new decision. Reassess your goal. If you want to stick to it, then reassess your strategy. Break the goal down into smaller or more manageable chunks. Call an accountability buddy or cheerleader who can help you jumpstart. Just get moving. You have not failed; you are learning more about yourself and your needs and interests.

Pressure Points

Sometimes you will notice that you keep running into the same problem. The way to deal with reoccurring problems or **pressure points** is by planning, which is a big part of training. A runner plans for the difficult stages of a race, and a mom needs to plan for her pressure points. To do this, first identify one or two problem times that cause stress on a regular basis. Write them on a piece of paper. Now write the activities that usually precede and follow that activity. What can you do to push back the preceding activity? What can you do to push forward the following activity? If the following activity is a "hard" start time, like school, list TWO things that precede the problem time.

Now look at the surrounding activities. What could you do to give yourself more time at the pressure point? Perhaps the answer is as simple as getting the kids up ten minutes earlier or having the kids pack their lunches the previous night. Only you can say what you can and can't do. Use a chart like the one below to see how the pressure point builds up and how you can release some of the pressure.

Problem: Need Extra Time

Pre/Post Problem	Push Back/Forward Strategy	Time Gained
Breakfast	Set the table the night before and put the cereals on the table	10 min.
Dress	Get the kids to choose school clothes the night before	10 min.

This strategy can also be used for special cases. If you know that you have a rough day coming up, PLAN FOR IT. Ask another mother to do carpool duty or hire a sitter or ask a friend to help you out. Remember: friends are willing to help out when you need them, but they can't read your mind!

Streamlining Your Day and Week

If you are going in a hundred directions, you can feel scattered and drained. If you streamline your energy by getting a little more organized, you can save yourself some time and angst. Your strategic plan gives you a game plan and helps you to edit your schedule. I have also already talked about identifying pressure points and working with those. Now how about introducing some other practical systems into your household and daily life?

Where else can you and your family save some time? The moms I interviewed had lots of ideas.

Remember, these are lists of ideas. There is a lot here, so don't get overwhelmed. Try one idea for a while when you are up for it. See if it works in your family. If it doesn't, then try another. For example, I am planning to try out the weekly meal menu one of these days, but I am not ready to do so yet. Instead, I am going to start with using a slow cooker. It is cold outside and we are looking for hot meals anyway.

- **Meal Menus** — Many moms swear by these. Some print the menu out on Sundays for the week so that everyone knows what is for dinner and how they can help prepare the food. Others choose theme nights such as Monday is vegetarian, Tuesday is pasta, Wednesday is ethnic, Thursday is meat, and so on through the week. Some use meal-planning cookbooks such as *Saving Dinner: The Menus, Recipes, and Shopping Lists to Bring Your Family Back to the Table* by Leanne Ely. Other moms use websites for planning meals such as www.meals.com, which has over 15,000 recipes and a handy "Meal Plan Central" button linked to meal plans and grocery lists for the week.

- **Grocery Shopping** — Some moms keep weekly computerized shopping lists with the most frequently purchased items handy, making additions as needed. Online home delivery services like www.Safeway.com can be a boon for busy moms and are replete with personalized shopping lists, though some people prefer to pick out their own produce. Before traveling anywhere in the country, you can order nonperishable food, diapers, and formula up to a week in advance from www.netgrocer.com and have your items waiting for you upon your arrival.

- **Cooking Days** — A designated weekend cooking day helps many working moms get ready for the week and keeps daily dinner prep to a minimum so that they can come home from work and have food on the table within twenty or thirty minutes. A big cooking day every other week can dovetail with potlucks, teacher appreciation commitments, or meals for the community. Use what you need and freeze the rest. Slow cookers are back and have great recipe books such as Phyllis Pellman Good's *Fix-It & Forget-It Lightly:*

Healthy Low-Fat Recipes for Your Slow Cooker or the more traditional Betty Crocker's *Slow Cooker Cookbook*. Some quick prep in the a.m. and you'll have a fabulous hot dinner in the p.m.

- **Meals to Community** — Get large aluminum or plastic containers at Costco, Wal-Mart, Sam's Club, etc., so that you do not have to worry about retrieving your special cookware and Tupperware. If you have enough trouble just getting meals on your own table but do want to help out, create a Trader Joe's or Whole Foods basket of goodies such as yummy pasta, sauce, salad kit, fresh bread, and a dessert item. The recipient family can quickly cook it at their leisure.

- **School Lunch Strategies** — You can make lunches the night before. Put lettuce in a zip lock so that bread does not get soggy. One mom makes PB&Js, the only sandwich her son will eat, for the week on Sunday night and freezes them. They are thawed by lunchtime. Another mom uses a storage bin for assorted lunch snacks. A child can pick a snack for the day out of the bin in the kitchen. Others do assembly lines with kids in the morning, or make sandwiches and drinks and have kids pick an item from a fruit bowl, vegetable bin, and snack jar and put it in their lunch box. Still others create regular weekly combinations out of the available options such as: two school lunches, two homemade lunches, and one Lunchable per week. This puts kids and moms on the same page. For some creative and nutritious lunch ideas see www.wholefoodsmarket.com and go to "kids' recipes," which includes cool fuel for kids and a handy lunch box primer. *The Healthy Body Cookbook: Over 50 Fun Activities and Delicious Recipes for Kids* by Joan D'Amico and Karen Eich Drummond not only includes popular kid-tested recipes and fun educational activities, but also addresses safety in the kitchen. Klutz also has some fun twists on the boring school lunch.

- **Systems in House** — Create designated spots for phone lists, homework, library books, athletic gear, transitional papers, etc. You can use folders, bags, drawers, or baskets. An excellent handbook for any mom is Donna Smallin's *The One-Minute Organizer: Plain and Simple*, which boasts of "500 Tips for Getting Your Life in Order." Part One features "Getting Organized" and Part Two is filled with tips and strategies on "Staying Organized." She is also the author of *Organizing Plain and Simple*. You can also go to www.flylady.com for many handy organizational tricks and tips as well as encouragement.

- **Family Calendar** — Place a large wall calendar in a high traffic area of the house such as the kitchen. Give everyone his or her own color pen or color code by activity.

- **Family Resource Binder** — Create a binder with all pertinent family, medical, and activity information as well as necessary directions. It can also include family schedules. This binder can be used by family members, sitters, grandparents, etc. Keep binder handy in kitchen for easy access.

- **Systems in the Car** — You can put storage bins in the car: one for nonperishable snacks and drinks, another for sunscreen, bug spray, spare clothes, sweaters, and a third for playground toys or spare equipment. Have other bins labeled for each child in the garage so each child has his or her own for helmets, pads, rollerblades, etc. You can pull any bin out and put in the car as needed. Gear returns right back to the bin after the sport.

- **Prepacked Activity Bags** — These are great for travel, sports fields, or restaurants. Pack them with age-appropriate items such as markers, paper, coloring books, a deck of cards, travel games, container of small critters or dolls or paperback books. Pull out as needed. Some moms keep one handy in the car, others in a closet or the garage.

- **Activity/Sport Handouts** — You can have a hanging file system in the kitchen for easy access for all family members. Some moms put it in a basket. Another handy system is to have a three-ringed binder already filled with plastic page protectors. As essential sports and school handouts come home, slip them in. You can keep the binder in the kitchen, but some moms want it in the car so that if it is sprinkling and soccer might be cancelled, the rain hotline and information is at their fingertips.

For more tips and strategies on home organization, weekly meal planning and creative school lunches, go to Resources at www.sportofmotherhood.com.

Recap

- Review your Strategic Plan from Chapter 3.
- Run any potential commitment through your **EFFECT** list and see if it is still right for you.
- Pick ONE goal and put your plan aside for the time being.
- Start by taking one step at a time.
- Apply the **Minimum/Bonus Strategy**.
- Evaluate progress daily or weekly as time allows.

Wrap-Up

As you begin to train for your daily and weekly goal, you will run into some obstacles and hit some walls. What happens to your morale and efforts then? Do you want to throw in the towel or keep moving? You might have sore muscles and just need to stretch a bit more or even take a little time off. Maybe you just need a boost of humor or perspective, and then you are on your way again.

If you want some extra practice with identifying commitments that drain or add energy, then work through the exercises below. Otherwise, let's move on to Chapter 6, which looks at finding endurance, faith and insight.

EXERCISES

Warm Up: Reflective Stretches

List two examples of areas in your life that involve clutter (material items or commitments).

1. _____
2. _____

When you think of tackling the clutter, how do you feel? Write down your response.

_____

Before taking on a new commitment, do you typically (circle the answers that apply to you):

a. Assess whether or not you have the time? **Yes or No**
b. Ask yourself why you would want to take on a new commitment? **Yes or No**
c. Ask for details regarding what is involved? **Yes or No**
d. Check your calendar? **Yes or No**
e. Run it by a friend, partner or accountability buddy? **Yes or No**
f. Take another commitment off your list? **Yes or No**
g. Assess the tone in your home? (Is anyone sick or troubled, traveling a lot with work? Are you in a particularly busy stage of parenting?) **Yes or No**

How many **Yes** answers did you circle? Compare your total with the score below and see if you are:

0–1   Flying by the seat of your pants
2–3   Making headway
4–5   Prioritizing with some purpose and intentionality
6–7   Streamlining like a pro

List two examples of phrases you use to say "No" to taking on a new commitment:

1. _____
2. _____

Practice: New Skills

1. Assess your energy. Fill in the table below and see what you learn. Be sure to include activities that you would like to do or have been asked to do.

Energy Table

Which activities give you energy?	Which activities drain your energy?

2. Learn to Say "No" to others and "Yes" to yourself. This applies to all nonessential requests for your time, including volunteer commitments. Fill in the table below. Get creative with your responses!

Saying "No" Table

Examples of Saying "No"	Your Personal Examples of Saying "No"
Thank you, but my plate is full right now.	
I cannot commit now, but maybe next year (or next season).	
Let me sleep on it.	
I need to check with my husband (or partner) and get back to you.	
I have just checked my calendar and can only add if I edit, which I can't do right now.	
I will get back to you in 24 hours.	
I need to pass this time, but thanks for thinking of me.	

3. Assess new commitments. Take any potential new commitment through the EFFECT list before you accept it. Write your responses below.

Prioritize Commitments Using EFFECT

- Evaluate — the commitment
- Fits — fits in your current strategic plan or schedule
- Fits — fits with your abilities
- Edit — edit your current to-do list
- Confess — why consider this commitment
- Tone — what is current tone in home? Positive and full of energy, or low because of sickness?

List the possible commitment.

_____

    a. Evaluate, what is required: _____

    b. Fits current plan/schedule? (Circle answer) **Yes or No**

    c. Fits abilities (or talents)? (Circle answer) **Yes or No**

    d. Edit current to-do list (where?) _____

    e. Confess (why take this on?): _____

    f. Tone in home (current)? _____

4. Identify pressure points. Use the table below to identify a typical daily or weekly pressure point and plan for it. Fill in the blank table below after reading the example.

Identify Pressure Points Example

Pre/Post Problem	Push Back/Forward Strategy	Time Gained
Breakfast	Set the table the night before and put the cereals on the table	10 min.
Dress	Lay out clothes night before school	10 min.
Carpool snacks	Keep bin in car stocked with non-perishables/waters	10 min.

Identify Pressure Points (YOUR TABLE)

Pre/Post Problem	Push Back/Forward Strategy	Time Gained

Cool Down

1. List one item that you can take off of your to-do list or schedule.

_____

2. List one way that you can streamline your week or combine activities, meals, or schedules.

_____

CHAPTER 6

Pacing and Endurance for Moms

> ▶ R U stuck or N a rut?
> ▶ Would U like a good belly laugh + benefit from injecting some humor into your daily life?
> ▶ R U short on some good attitude?

By training for your objectives and streamlining your schedule, you are pacing yourself for your day and your week. If your goals are manageable and your pace reasonable, you can stay on course for life, assessing and adapting as needed. To reach that steady state, it's important to periodically review your training schedule and note how you feel. Touch base with yourself regularly, and you'll learn how to pace yourself for the long run ahead.

Sometimes you may be doing too many good things and are just too busy. You may begin to feel overwhelmed, over-stretched, or anxious. Your patience dwindles. When this happens, your pace is too fast and you are setting yourself up for hitting walls. If you train yourself to detect the warning signs early on, you can be ready to adapt your training, edit your schedule, take some downtime, and refuel as needed without getting too far off course.

Sore Muscles

What happens when you develop sore muscles? When a runner is pushing to increase her endurance or does weight training, her sore muscles are a signal of increasing strength. It doesn't feel good at the time, but it can be a sign of progress. At other times, the soreness just doesn't seem to go away. When that happens, she may be pushing her body too hard. As you train, be alert for sore muscles signaling that you are doing too much. Maybe you just can't seem to get enough done, or you are too darn cranky in the evening, or you just feel like throwing in the towel. Feelings of depletion may be a sign that your training schedule is no longer appropriate. Only you can know what your body is telling you. Perhaps you need to back off a bit. You can rest, try something new, and adapt as needed. Remember, your training schedule is there to serve you. You shouldn't feel like you are chasing it. With the right pacing, training feels good.

The best way to deal with pacing is by assessing where you are and where you want to go. Are your goals still realistic or are you pushing too hard? Here are some tips and tools that can help you figure that out.

Pacing and Assessment Tips and Tools

- **Honestly Assess Your Current Status.** Check in every so often and ask yourself, "How am I feeling?" If you have less patience, feel snappy with others, feel like you don't have the time to sit and breathe, or have lost the joy, then it is probably time to edit your or your family's schedule. You can also work on one goal and then shift to another. Ebb and flow. The goal calendar is meant to help you, not be a burden.

- **Respect Your Threshold.** You may get ideas from others, but only you know when you are getting close to your limit. We all have different needs and body rhythms. What works for one person may not work for another. Some people need more sleep, some less. Some people don't want any commitments outside of family; some thrive on them.

- **Be Flexible and Adapt.** Mothers, by definition, live in the midst of constant change. Our children grow and change, our families change and so does the balance of our lives as mothers. A schedule that works for a few months may need to adapt to new criteria: a new pregnancy, the health of someone in the family, a particularly challenging developmental stage in one of the kids, accidents, job changes, new school schedules, additional responsibilities. . . . You may need to alter your weekly goals. In fact, you can expect to alter them.

- **Listen to Your Heart.** Sometimes, things will seem to be fine intellectually, but your heart feels heavy. What are you missing? Take a walk, sit under a tree, or simply have a quiet cup of tea and be silent. Think about the heaviness you are feeling and see if you can identify the cause. Perhaps one of your kids needs extra attention, or because of your training you've been postponing an outing that you promised the kids. If you take the time to listen, your heart will usually speak and tell you what is wrong. Knowing the obstacle is the first step in overcoming it.

- **Train a Week at a Time.** No single day has to be perfect. Just as our pediatricians tell us to review a toddler's diet over the course of a whole week for adequate nutrition, you can find your equilibrium over the course of a week. If you have to skip some of your goal time one day, you can try to make all or part of it up another day. If you can't make up the actual time, good concentration one day is just as good. A week gives you more leeway for meeting your goals.

- **Keep or Create Down Time.** You need it. Everyone needs it to different degrees. Some moms need to schedule it in or call it "me time." Others seek it and take advantage of it as it happens. Do what works for you, but protect your time to recharge. If you sit still and let your mind clear, you will feel more grounded.

- **Set Boundaries.** Just as a runner has a particular course to run, you too can limit the diversions in your day. Protect your family time and your goal time when you can. Check in with an accountability buddy if you want a little permission to let yourself off the hook. (Believe it or not, this does help!) Sometimes you are too close to what you are doing to see what a friend can easily identify. Use your support network; that's what it is there for! Draw some boundaries around computer time for yourself if you feel addicted to email or work (paid or volunteer), which can spill over into family time.

- **Use a Goal Journal.** Pull out your Goal Journal. Write down how your training is going and what you might change. How does your pace feel? Is anything blocking you? A goal journal is a great record, and gives you the information to make informed decisions as you define future objectives and plans. You can always look back to see how you "trained" for one goal, and how you felt about different aspects of the training.

> **MOM TIP**
>
> I keep a writing journal. In it, I note how I am feeling during different stages of my writing, ranging from frustrated to euphoric—maybe all in one day. I note what else is going on in my life and how it influences my energy and focus. The journal helps me to see the big picture, to more effectively pace myself and to edit my training schedule as I work towards my writing goals.

Attitude Boosters

Life is full of challenges and mishaps. Attitude is a key to happiness, and your attitude is something you can really influence. Try to view each challenge as an adventure or a learning experience. An obstacle course can be fun. Sometimes, even when you are facing a calamity, you will note the support of friends, amazing coincidences, or small miracles around you. Perhaps your faith deepens as you learn to let go a little bit.

> **MOM TIP**
>
> We can't control life, but we can make choices with our actions and reactions. If we have had a challenging day at work, with the kids, or with a nasty driver on the freeway, we can choose to "start our day over," appreciate our humanness and find an opportunity for personal growth.

I have put together an attitude toolkit to help you find and maintain that good state of mind—you know, the one that turns the lemons into lemonade. This kit contains five tools: perspective, affirmations, daily readings, humor, and gratitude journals.

1. Perspective

Sometimes my kids and I have to start the day over five times. Take a deep breath and try to clear your head. As you exhale, visualize a new beginning: ocean waves washing back from the beach, a soft rain, high clouds against a blue sky; whatever speaks to you. Give yourself and those around you a chance to begin the day over with a better outlook and attitude. Don't get caught up in living in the past or the future or you'll miss the beauty of now. Each day is precious. Enjoy the ride!

> **MOM TIP**
>
> You can start your day over as many times as you like.

> **MOM TIP**
>
> Another easy boost is to ask your kids each night what kind or generous things they did that day. The first time or two they may have trouble coming up with one. Over time, they'll start identifying and doing more kind things for others.

Help someone else to get some perspective. This is so effective. You can even do this with your kids. There are both formal and informal community outreach programs through schools, churches and your community. You can visit nursing homes (if all kids are well) or make something for an older neighbor down the street. Your kids can help serve some meals at the local homeless shelter or create Easter baskets for those in need. Bring a meal to someone who just had a baby. You can do a little bit here and there or volunteer regularly. Your kids will also pick up on the good vibes and the gift of giving.

> **MOM TIP**
> Some moms I interviewed think of the children with special needs that they see every day, and others think of global concerns and war. Compared to issues like these, their daily challenges feel small. These moms do not believe their own problems are unworthy; rather they have just gained some important perspective.

2. Affirmations

You know that tiny voice that says you can't do something, or of course you aren't good at something? You can train yourself not to listen to your inner critic. One way to counteract this negativity is through affirmations or repeated short sentences or phrases that affirm you in whatever capacity that you need or want. Affirmations can help you to create a positive attitude. Some enthusiasts even recommend writing down the negative thoughts, ripping them up, and putting them in the trash. Mentally, you are done with them and are making room for the new ones. Affirmations can help you to eliminate the negative talk in your own head and serve to unblock your spirit and purpose.

Begin with short phrases that build on positive character traits or talents such as: I am healthy, loving and kind. I am strong. I have resilience or tenacity. I am skilled. I am creative. I can create. You can also say, "I have hope" or "I am willing" if you are struggling with a change.

> **Mom Story**
> The affirmation "I am enough" can help you reframe your day and see that your cup is half full. Whether we have one, two, three, or more kids, mothers can feel inadequate as a mother, as a wife, as an employee, or contributor to the community or the world at large. I know that saying "I am enough" helps me to focus on what I can do and am already doing. I use it when I hear the negative banter in my head. I have also learned to think "this is enough" when our house feels too small for six bodies. We are lucky to have a home. "This is enough" inspires me to get rid of clutter and streamline as much as possible.

Think about the negative tapes that you play in your head. Sometimes these thoughts are so familiar that we don't even hear them anymore. Change each negative into a positive. If you are critical of your looks, then look in the mirror and say, "I am beautiful," "I am healthy," or "I like my nose." Make a list of the qualities that you admire in yourself and read it often. If you are dealing with change or juggling a lot of balls, you can say things like: I have stamina, I am organized, I can do this one step at a time, I can breathe, I can reach out, I can let go, I am open, I have energy, I am clear-thinking or insightful, I have patience or I have support. Tailor the affirmation to your specific need.

Be creative. Borrow lines from those who inspire you. Lines and stanzas of songs can be turned into affirmations. Jana Stanfield has a song called "More Than Enough" that inspires many people.

> I have more than enough,
> Of all that I need,
> To do all I can do,
> Be all I can be.

Here is a line in another one of her songs: "I cannot do all the good that the world needs, but the world needs all the good I can do." To find out more about Jana Stanfield's songs, go to her website at www.janastanfield.com. Volume 4, "Let the Change Begin," is particularly inspiring and can provide a much-needed boost to your spirits.

You can also add more words to your affirmation to come up with a phrase. Corie reminds herself, "Don't take it personally." Alana often uses "One thing at a time" to keep her on track. "One day at a time or one minute at a time" draws from twelve-step groups, and is useful and popular.

There are a number of useful affirmation websites. Gems for Friends at www.gems4friends.com not only has affirmation techniques, exercises and a free monthly newsletter, but also includes links to Affirmations or Inspiration of the Day quotes and an annotated bibliography of inspirational books. The site's Affirmations of the Day tend to be short and manageable, such as: I am a unique and wonderful individual; I eat right, exercise, and take great care of my body; I am wise; I breathe in love every moment. This way you can remember them and say them throughout the day.

WomanLinks.com, subtitled "Well-behaved women rarely make history," has Daily Affirmations along with Attitude Adjusters, a chat room, and topic-related online postings. Go to www.womanlinks.com/affirmations.html for more information. If you seek new ways to create your own affirmations, go to the exercises at the end of this chapter. You can also use Julia Cameron's *The Artist's Way*, Susan Jeffers's *Dare to Connect: How to Create Confidence, Trust and Loving Relationships*, and Eric Maisel's *The Creativity Book: A Year's Worth of Inspiration and Guidance* as additional resources.

> **MOM TIP**
>
> "We try to raise our children in unconditionally loving households; why not do the same for ourselves? Just as children do not thrive under criticism and sarcasm, neither do we." —Jill

If we replace the negative tapes in our head with positive ones, we will find new strengths, joy, and perspective. Guaranteed! You may feel silly at first, but give it a shot for three weeks—yes, I am back to the three-week trial period again. Just do it and see what happens.

Some Tips for Using Affirmations

- Set aside five to ten minutes every day to affirm who you are, what you can do, or what you want to be able to do.
- Say them as you exercise, drive the car, take the bus, brush your teeth, vacuum your house . . . you get the picture.
- Say them when you get down on yourself, or just need a boost of courage to be who you are or want to be.
- Say them (to yourself) when you are in the middle of an irritating disagreement with someone. You can't change them, but you can change your dance, attitude, or reactions.
- Write them down and make them feel like they are yours.
- Post them on your refrigerator, mirror, car dashboard, or the inside cover of your appointment book.

Use them regularly and your attitude *will* change.

3. Daily Readings

Daily reading books with either meditations or inspirational passages and quotes can be a boon to a sagging attitude or just keep you on the right track. When you pick up one of these books, you choose to start your day—or reframe a day—with a good dose of perspective. Books such as Anne Wilson Schaef's *Meditations for Women Who Do Too Much*, Michelle Medlock Adams' *Daily Wisdom for Mothers: A 365-Day Devotional*, and *Hazeldon's Each Day a New Beginning: Daily Meditations for Women* by Karen Casey can help you get grounded and stay focused throughout your day. Sarah Ban Breathnach's *Simple Abundance: A Daybook of Comfort and Joy* is also an inspiring daily reader. You can also access helpful hints and sayings at her website www.simpleabundance.com.

How about going to The Daily Motivator at www.greatday.com/motivate where you can receive a Daily Motivator each day via email? The site also offers Daily Motivator Music and Videos. If you are looking for more religious fuel, then Daily Scripture Readings & Meditations at www.rc.net/wcc/readings could be for you, depending on your religion.

You could also go to Meditation Tip of the Day at www.deeshan.com, which represents daily meditations from a variety of sources and religions. DailyOM is popular. Just go to www.dailyom.com to sign up for your Daily Meditations. You can even publish DailyOM on your website to give viewers a boost. If you are having trouble letting go, practicing meditations or keeping it simple, Jon Kabat-Zinn's *Wherever You Go, There You Are: Mindfulness Meditation in Everyday Life* can help you get into the meditation mindset.

Some mothers like to get up ten minutes early to do their meditation and set the tone for the day. Others pull out their guiding books, palm pilots, or computers whenever they have the opportunity. Try both approaches, or try a combination of the two to see what works best for you with your particular schedule and family dynamic. Don't be afraid to experiment and *keep trying* until you find something that works.

4. Humor: The Ultimate Attitude Adjuster

Humor can turn both your and your family's mood around. Where do you find your humor? Call a friend. Remind yourself that tomorrow it will be funny. My family and I love the comics. *Baby Blues*, *Sally Forth*, *Dennis the Menace*, *Zits*, and *Family Circus* comic strips resonate with me as I raise my family. Especially *Baby Blues*. The authors Rick Kirkman and Jerry Scott just get all the zaniness, fun, trials and loss of perspective parents experience while raising little kids.

We also get silly and substitute silly words in favorite songs. I had one child who would cling to my leg and become mute when encountering adults. So I often introduced her as "Peanut Butter" and her brother as "Jelly." It worked every time. She would laugh, say "NOOOOO, that's not it," and tell them her real name.

Sam, a mom, finds that "when my children are fixated on something or in a sour mood, I try to shift their attention if possible, sometimes by asking a nonsense-type question, one that shakes them up. Lately a tension-breaker has been to play 'rock, paper, scissors' (as silly as it may sound, but my kids are little so they like it). Or sometimes we sing the 'name game' song ("Michael, Michael, Bo Bichael, Banana Fanna Fo Fichael . . ."). My children like Shel Silverstein's poetry because it's silly. . . . They love to be tickled. . . . They get a huge kick out of playing hide and seek. . . there is a lot of laughter when we play."

Find the humor, even if it is only for your own benefit. One mom talked about the time when her kids acted up while she stood in a long grocery line. She got creative and said to the people behind her, "This is the last time I'm taking care of my neighbor's kids!" When you make a mistake or are stuck in an unfavorable situation, try to laugh about it. If a mishap is especially wrenching or exasperating at the time, it will be funny later—guaranteed!

Others families find humor in listening to funny tapes (by Jim Copp, for example), reading joke books, or visiting funny websites, such as www.garfield.com, www.neopets.com. If you want more ideas, ask your kids what they find funny. Disregarding potty humor, you might learn something new.

Humor emails can be a boost. Keep a file of favorites for yourself or to pass along to others. How about this Mammogram Ditty that recently made the email rounds:

HAVE YOUR MAMMIES GRAMMED

For years and years they told me,
Be careful of your breasts.
Don't ever squeeze or bruise them.
And give them monthly tests.

So I heeded all their warnings,
And protected them by law.
Guarded them very carefully,
And I always wore my bra.

After 30 years of astute care,
My gynie, Dr. Pruitt,
Said I should get a Mammogram
"O.K," I said, "let's do it."

"Stand up here real close" she said,
(She got my boob in line),
"And tell me when it hurts," she said,
"Ah yes! Right there, that's fine."

She stepped upon a pedal,
I could not believe my eyes!
A plastic plate came slamming down,
My hooter's in a vise!

My skin was stretched and mangled,
From underneath my chin.
My poor boob was being squashed,
To Swedish Pancake thin.

Excruciating pain I felt,
Within its vise-like grip.

A prisoner in this vicious thing,
My poor defenseless tit!

"Take a deep breath" she said to me,
Who does she think she's kidding?!?
My chest is mashed in her machine,
And woozy I am getting.

"There, that's good," I heard her say,
(The room was slowly swaying.)
"Now, let's have a go at the other one."
Have mercy, I was praying.

It squeezed me from both up and down,
It squeezed me from both sides.
I'll bet SHE'S never had this done,
To HER tender little hide.

Next time that they make me do this,
I will request a blindfold.
I have no wish to see again,
My knockers getting steam-rolled.

If I had no problem when I came in,
I surely have one now.
If there had been a cyst in there,
It would have gone "ker-pow!"

This machine was created by a man,
Of this, I have no doubt.
I'd like to stick his balls in there,
And see how THEY come out!

Or another one:

Dear Tech Support,

Last year I upgraded from Boyfriend 5.0 to Husband 1.0 and noticed a distinct slowdown in overall system performance—particularly in the flower and jewelry applications, which operated flawlessly under Boyfriend 5.0.

In addition, installation of Husband 1.0 seems to have uninstalled many other valuable programs, such as Romance 9.5 and Personal Attention 6.5, and then installed such other undesirable programs as NFL 5.0, NBA 3.0 and Golf Clubs 4.1. Conversation 8.0 no longer runs, and Housecleaning 2.6 simply crashes the system. I've tried running Nagging 5.3 to fix these problems, but to no avail. What can I do?

Signed,
Desperate

Dear Desperate,

First keep in mind that Boyfriend 5.0 is an Entertainment Package, while Husband 1.0 is an Operating System. Please enter the command: "http: I Thought You Loved Me . . . htm" and try to download Tears 6.2, and don't forget to install the Guilt 3.0 update. If that application works as designed, Husband 1.0 should then automatically run the applications Jewelry 2.0 and Flowers 3.5. But remember, overuse of the above application can cause Husband 1.0 to default to Grumpy Silence 2.5, Happy Hour 7.0, or Beer 6.1. Beer 6.1 is a very bad program that will automatically download the Snoring Loudly Beta.

Whatever you do, DO NOT install Mother-in-law 1.0 (it runs a virus in the background which will eventually seize control of all your system resources). Also, do not attempt to reinstall the Boyfriend 5.0 program. This is an unsupported application and will crash Husband 1.0.

In summary, Husband 1.0 is a great program, but it does have limited memory and cannot learn new applications quickly. You might consider buying additional software to improve memory and performance. We recommend Hot Food 3.0 and Lingerie 7.7.

Good Luck,
Tech Support

Those really got me laughing. How about you? You can always go to joke websites such as Jokes-n-Fun.com at www.jokes-n-fun.com, which has jokes listed by category such as animal, children, medical, sports and one-line jokes categories as well as real school note bloopers such as: "Please excuse Jennifer for missing school yesterday. We forgot to get the Sunday paper off the porch, and when we found it Monday, we thought it was Sunday." Jokes-n-Fun.com states on the site that it "takes pride in providing jokes on the Internet that are appropriate for the entire family. All of the children jokes on this site have been reviewed for content. All of the children jokes are clean and funny."

You can even sign up for a joke a day through a popular site such as Joke-of-the-Day.com at www.joke-of-the-day.com. Billed as the world's largest daily joke list, Joke-of-the-Day.com also offers joke categories and cartoons and does not bombard you with advertisements. Both sites are in Yahoo's "most popular" list. If you are up for brainteasers go to www.todayschuckle.com and click on the teasers or puzzles links.

Looking for more? Of course, Yahooligans at www.yahooligans.com is the ultimate web guide and educational resource for kids. It has humor links such as jokes and games, but also it has music, cool sites, news, science, reference, and "Ask Earl" links. More still? Go to the Yahoo Entertainment Directory in the "Joke a Day" category at www.dir.yahoo.com/Entertainment/Humor/Jokes/Joke_of_the_Day or by doing a Google search under "joke a day."

If you are sending out humor emails, try to keep your audience's tastes in mind. Bombarding someone with political or sexual jokes may not be someone else's idea of a good time.

5. Gratitude Journals

Believe it or not, they work. If you need a morale booster, write down all that you are grateful for in your journal. You can do this daily or occasionally, when the mood strikes. If you don't feel like writing a list down or you don't have a pen and paper, simply say the list in your head. Find a quiet time at the end of the day and go through your blessings, from your own health to the health of those around you. If you are sick or you are anxious about a child's sickness, find something to be grateful for: the doctors, medical care, the health of the rest of your family, new support, new or deepened faith, etc. Get back to the basics: food and shelter over your head, a yummy meal, a special time with a child, your partner, a friend, and so forth.

Wrap-Up

Pacing is all about making an honest assessment of where you are and then figuring what you need to do to get from there to where you want to be. By setting boundaries, keeping reasonable goals and creating down time, you'll be more likely to succeed. Be flexible enough to change when needed, so you can pace yourself and stay the course in this new adventure.

When your attitude sags, buoy it up with a change of perspective. Try affirmations, inspiration, and humor. Journals can help you to monitor your progress or remember all the reasons you have to be thankful. All these tools together will keep you moving forward. Unfortunately, there will always be times when situations hit us like a tidal wave and we are left adrift in a mess. That's when you need the resources I describe in the next chapter, Chapter 7: Hitting Walls and Bouncing Back.

EXERCISES

If you would like some additional practice with creating your own affirmations and expanding your attitude toolkit, then try these exercises.

Warm Up: Reflective Stretches

1. List two hobbies or interests that you have thought about adding to your life when you have more time.

   a. _____

   b. _____

2. When you think of tackling a new endeavor, how do you feel? Write it down.

   _____

3. Before trying something new, do you (circle the answers that apply to you):

   a. Worry about making a fool of yourself? **Yes or No**
   b. Wonder what would happen if you fail? **Yes or No**
   c. Feel like you "should" do it because others expect you too? **Yes or No**
   d. Think of other times you have messed up or not succeeded with original goal? **Yes or No**
   e. Feel nervous about trying it alone? **Yes or No**
   f. Get excited to dive in but don't know where to start? **Yes or No**
   g. Doubt your abilities or your follow-through? **Yes or No**
   h. Find it better not to try at all than to not complete project or goal? **Yes or No**

How many **Yes** answers did you circle? Compare your total with the score below and see where you stand:

   0–2 Hot dog. You define success by trying.
   3–4 Nerves test your spirit. You could benefit from an accountability buddy or class to get you to commit.
   5–6 The Fool Factor has you in its grips, but you will put your toe in the water.
   7–8 Missing out on some real fun.

4. List two doubts you have about your mental, physical or social abilities.

   a. _____
   b. _____

Practice: New Skills

Evaluate Your Pacing

1. Do you ever stop to ask, "How am I feeling?" **Yes or No**
2. Do you often take on one more project or committee that spreads you a little too thin? **Yes or No**

3. When you are tight on time, do you (circle the answers that apply to you):

    a. bark at the next person in your path? **Yes or No**

    b. snap at a family member later in the day? **Yes or No**

    c. stop to breathe? **Yes or No**

    d. find a way to edit the schedule? **Yes or No**

4. Do you feel like you are on a treadmill and cannot get off? **Yes or No**

5. Are there things you want to do but can't find the time until work slows down or the kids are older? **Yes or No**

6. Are you having much fun lately? **Yes or No**

Evaluate Your Quality of Life

Understand your own thresholds to establish a good quality of life.

1. Sleep

    How much sleep do you like to get? _____

    How much sleep do you actually get? _____

    How much sleep do you need? _____

2. Volunteer commitments: Do you like to be involved in a number of activities or do one or two things in more depth? _____

3. Which elements factor into your decision-making when faced with optional commitments (circle the answers that apply to you)?

    a. fits in schedule

    b. involves family

    c. involves personal or career growth

    d. involves socializing with other adults to help keep you connected

    e. makes other people happy

    f. takes a burden off of others

Evaluate Your Time Management

1. List one goal or dream on which you want to focus. _____
2. Write down your realistic weekly minimum (hours/events/classes per week) for this goal. _____
3. List three things that count as time spent on this goal (includes research and prep time).

   _____, _____, _____

Wishes and Obstacles: I Want to, But . . .

1. Make a Wish List: think of two things you want to try or learn how to do.

   _____, _____

2. Obstacles: List two things that stop you from trying something that you want to do or learn how to do.

   _____, _____

3. Name your worst critic. _____

Create Topic-Related Affirmations

If you want some more ideas for affirmations that are applicable to your situation, then look through the following categories and lists. Use them verbatim or as springboards for your own ideas.

Category: Motherhood. I am: loving, loved, kind, nurturing, honest, responsible, creative, energized, alive, trusting, strong, joyful, patient, fun, funny, playful, open, flexible, adaptable, enough

Category: Creativity. I am: an artist, a writer, a dancer, a listener, a channel, inspired, enthusiastic, bold, passionate, driven, human, creative, strong, focused, tenacious, carefree, playful, serious, pensive, steady, patient

Category: Personal Health. I am: healthy, responsible, disciplined, strong, fit, active, energized, calm, rested, alert, sober, full

Category: Faith. I can: believe, meditate, pray, be open, be willing to be open, try, ask for help or guidance, be disciplined about my studies

1. Your Categories: _____
2. Your Examples: _____

Create Short Affirmations

Go back to your **Wish List** and **Obstacles List**. Look over your answers. Now put together three or four words that are positive (hint: opposite of negative), and work with your specific wishes and obstacles. You can use these affirmations to pull yourself up when you are doubting yourself. You can also read through the list below to get some ideas.

Courage, Faith, Action	Pain, Gain, Faith	Try, Move, Gain
Trust, Believe, Do	Loss, Life, Perspective	Free, Joy, Play
Peace, Love, Life	Attitude, Light, Joy	Try, Can, Do
Energy, Fire, Creativity	Listen, Discern, Speak	Courage, Mistakes, Learn
Dream, Vision, Plan	Give, Receive, Love	Negative, Affirm, Change
Understanding, Forgiving, Forgiven	Heart, Soul, Connection	Try, Practice, Progress
Prayer, Willingness, Open	Prayer, Action, Grounded	Faith, Listen, Purpose
Clear, Blank, Open	Still, Listen, Hear	Worry, Past, Possibilities, Future
Pause, Steady, Calm	Still, Refreshed, Spirit	I am enough.
Stop, Breathe, Listen	Blocked, Willing, Unblocked	This is enough.
Breathe, Pray, Shift	Down, Ask, Support	Just let go.
	Open, Heart, Mind	

Your Short Affirmations

_____, _____, _____
_____, _____, _____
_____, _____, _____
_____, _____, _____

Visualization Techniques

1. List two personal symbols (muse, bird soaring, inner lion).
   _____, _____

2. Imagine a calming image (beach, tides, bubble bath, etc.) or an energizing image to get you in the zone.

3. List one calming image. _____

4. List one energizing image. _____

5. Close your eyes. Take a few minutes to visualize a strong finish or a successful ending.

Cool-Down

1. List three possible times in your day that you could say short affirmations.
   _____, _____, _____

2. Write down three sources of humor that can boost your attitude (comics, joke-a-day, comedy, music/dance, etc., funny people).
   _____, _____, _____

3. List two people you know who laugh or smile a lot. Perhaps you can put people whom you find funny or fun in your life a bit more.
   _____, _____

CHAPTER 7

Hitting Walls and Bouncing Back

> ▶ R U able 2 identify red flags before U hit the wall or lose it?
> ▶ R U aware of any crash patterns N your daily or weekly life?
> ▶ When do U need 2 regroup + adjust expectations?

When a woman is out running a marathon, she has prepared herself to hit the wall. She's ready with a strategy for getting beyond the wall. In some races, she actually has a crowd cheering her on! Too often, a mom hits the wall unprepared, home alone with squalling or sick kids, relying completely on her love and imagination to get her through.

Mom Story

"One recent time . . . both of my kids were so cranky all day. The baby wouldn't sleep. The two-year-old was throwing one fit after another. I was at my wits' end. I couldn't even talk to anyone on the phone because somebody was always screaming in the background. And at one point in the afternoon I found myself carrying both of them, one screaming in each ear at the top of their lungs, slobbering on both of my shoulders, and I just lay down on my bed, with this screaming pile of kids on top of me, and I thought (half joking), 'Find your happy place, find your happy place.' But I could not get to 'my happy place' through

> screaming, slobbering, runny-nosed children. And I thought that maybe if I couldn't beat 'em, then I'd join 'em in crying. But before I broke, I just pictured what it must look like, me lying there numb on my bed with two screaming, slobbering, runny-nosed kids on top of me and how, if my husband came home right now, he would probably have to laugh before coming over to give me a hand, and it made me laugh too, or at least smile—well maybe—I didn't really smile, but I stopped being so grumpy about the whole thing, and got the energy back up to deal with them once again. And of course now I tell my friends about it and we sit back and laugh." —Tina

Tina had "hit the wall," or "spit the dummy" as one Australian mom described it. In a marathon, mile 18 is also known as the wall. The runner is tired and has 8.2 more miles to go. Going on seems impossible. The key is training: runners know about the mile 18 wall, so they train for it. When runners hit the wall, they have to regroup and adjust their attitude or expectations. When they do, what momentarily seemed like an impossible stretch becomes possible. They keep going.

Like runners, moms can train and prepare so that when they do hit the wall, they have the skills to get over it and keep on course. That said, moms face three unique challenges when training to get past tough spots. First, the walls that moms hit are not as predictable as mile 18, or as easily recognized. Sometimes they can be predicted, other times not. Kids are unpredictable, schedules are fluid, and moms are on call 24/7. Second, there's a double whammy for tired moms: when a mother hits the wall, her kids often fall apart or act out even more, amplifying the general distress. Children's sensory radars somehow tap into the mood. Third, dropping out of the race isn't an option for a mom. As a mom, you have to find a way to get through whatever you're facing. Your goal is to get through it as positively as possible.

In this chapter, we will take a look at situations that can force you to "the end of your rope." We'll explore what hitting the wall can feel like. By identifying triggers and getting rid of excess baggage, you can lighten your load and get past the wall. You can do this. Now let's talk about how.

How Do You Know When You Have "Hit the Wall"?

What does hitting the wall mean to you? It might mean losing patience or feeling out of control, helpless, overwhelmed, defeated, or depressed. When you hit a wall, you may think you can't keep going or get past it because you feel:

- **Helpless:** Sometimes we feel helpless when faced with adversity or some of life's big challenges. When Dena, a guest on *The Sport of Motherhood* TV Show, found out that her daughter was diagnosed with Asperger's, she felt helpless and overwhelmed. After a day or two of grieving shattered dreams, she gathered her wits and went into research mode, learning anything and everything she could about Asperger's. She became empowered and joked that she wanted to teach her whole preschool family class how to diagnose an Asperger's kid in under two minutes.

- **Out of Control:** Carrie, a stay-at-home mother of two who works from home, colorfully describes hitting the wall: "I try to pace myself, but inevitably, something happens to derail the pace—a business call, an explosive diaper, spilled milk, a temper tantrum, a child's illness or personal illness. . . . So much for 'the best laid plans.' As a result, I feel as though I am running around like a chicken with my head cut off." Prior to hitting the wall, she is aware of the change in her demeanor and attitude and is often able to do something about it. She says, "I feel it build up inside of me—it fills me up and then *I* have to take a time-out."

- **Impatient:** Karen, a full-time working mother of two, knows when she hits the wall because she loses "patience with my kids for doing things they are told not to do. Good parenting techniques for discipline go out the window, and I fall apart and yell." What does she do about it? "Apologize, try to

> **Mom Story**
>
> Emma aptly describes irritability: "I get snappy, short. I try to take a mental time-out to remember that my kids are just being kids, that God only gives us as much as we can handle. I have been doing a lot of reading on Buddhism and I find Buddhist philosophy very helpful for coping. I don't overcommit."

rewind the conversation, call my husband for a calmer parenting hand."

- **Unhappy:** Chaille, a working mother of two, finds she gets "really unhappy—grumpy, whiny, feel very put out. I usually talk about it, because that makes me feel better. I have people that I know I can whine to, and they can hear it and support me."

- **Loss of Perspective:** The little things start to get to Chris: "I know that I have 'hit the wall' when even the tiniest things are bugging me. I tend to either run my husband and kids out of the house, get involved with a 'cop' show, or I pack the whole family up in the car and we just drive somewhere."

- **Anxious:** Natalia, a full-time working mom of two, says, "I often 'hit the wall' near the end of each semester, when I have been immersed in work for an extended time, have not had a lot of sleep and am emotionally and psychically spent—all factors causing anxiety. When I am tired, I don't deal well with my own children when they whine or complain about something. If I have no free time except to fit in one outside activity, even if for one-half hour a week, exercise is my one savior. My mental health depends on it."

- **Mother's Guilt:** Margaret, another full-time working mother of two, says, "I always seem to be concerned about my children's behavior and I feel that expectations from my childhood (traditional British schooling) greatly influence my own expectations, even though, in principle, I don't think I value these expectations. I'm rarely as patient as I want to be, and this makes me feel incredibly guilty."

When they sat down to think and write about it, each of these women was able to recognize her internal signs that she had hit the wall. That is a great first step toward managing this emotional experience. If you can recognize your pattern, then you can start to anticipate when you are about to hit the wall. And if you can see the wall coming, you can do something about how you (and your kids) face the impact. You can prevent crisis and total meltdown.

There are many triggers that cause this feeling of "nevermore!" Let's look at some of the real repeaters. What are the common causes of hitting the wall for moms?

Hitting Walls and Bouncing Back

I group walls into three categories: **situational walls**, such as a bout of the chicken pox, a car breaking down, a computer crash, or a family gathering; **seasonal walls**, such as the beginning or end of school-year rush, tax time, or holiday madness; and **life-changing walls**, such as a chronic diagnosis, death, or divorce.

Life-changing walls hit you out of the blue, like a mudslide. They are unpredictable and huge. Situational and seasonal walls may taunt and tease you before they rear up in your path—you can often anticipate them, but they are still highly variable. Think of family gatherings you may be anxious about in advance, the flu season, or the busiest time of year at the office. They can also be unexpected, like a fender bender, a sprained ankle, or a forgotten birthday. I devote Chapter 8 to life-changing walls. In this chapter, we are going to focus on the identifying patterns, or red flags, that precede seasonal and situational walls. You can learn to recognize the patterns and train to face the walls with new skills.

What these walls look like and how you handle them vary from person to person. You will also find that you do have to update your tools: coping tools that worked during one stage of child-rearing may become partially or completely obsolete as your family grows and changes. Bat-Ami Klejner, a family therapist who was on *The Sport of Motherhood* TV show, advises mothers that "sometimes you need to do some spring cleaning and develop new coping skills—you need to clean out your toolbox, so to speak. You can do this on your own or get professional help during this transitional period" to accelerate the process.

Whether you are facing a particularly tiring day, a cranky toddler, an accident, or some of life's other adversities, you can use strategies, training, support networks, and allies to help you through. By identifying triggers before you hit a predictable wall, you can save yourself some frustration and have more energy to enjoy your family. Let's look at the red flags that often signal you are near a wall.

Red Flag: Feeling Fatigue

Fatigue is often a warning sign that you are about to hit the wall. Moms experience so much tiredness that they can get into the habit of ignoring it. Don't! Moms are programmed to go, go, go, and that can take you over. Try to listen to what your fatigue is telling you. Notice your own patterns. Are you tired at certain times of day, in certain situations? Here are some classic fatigue scenarios.

Your energy is gone. Just how do you face the afternoon stretch when you feel depleted? Whoever knew that time could move so slowly! What about surviving the "witching hour"? You know, the dinnertime hour when little ones are typically cranky and you are trying to prepare food for the table and feed the tribe.

Then there are the bedtime blues. You are already exhausted, when restless babies and toddlers or older children who cannot or will not go to sleep want your attention and just plain wear you out. You ask yourself, or your partner, or your dog: "Can't this day please be over?" You just want a good night's sleep and some time to recharge.

Dierdra, currently a mother of two who works part time, hit a wall with fatigue after her first child. One time after a long workday she "stopped at a light and realized that I could not tell if it was green or red—I was too exhausted." Her fatigue was a wake-up call. She was stretched too thin and decided right then to cut back her work hours.

Before they had their second child, Dierdra and her partner assessed their needs and division of responsibilities. "We identified balls that we could drop so that our sanity remained intact." She also "let go of some ideas I had before children," such as keeping an immaculate or organized house. She now makes "sure I get enough sleep so that I can function. When I am teaching, I go to bed around 8 p.m. We recognize that I need to give up my evening time with my husband, but we make up

Mom Story

Alexis, a mom of three, says she feels likes she is "breaking a mustang" as she teaches her willful six-year-old son some boundaries. "I am just wiped at the end of each day because of him." She says he is "so much fun but such an imp sometimes! He got three time-outs this afternoon for backtalk. What do you do with someone who doesn't care about a time-out? I finally brought out bright pink paper and wrote '– 15' when he acted up. He got three of those and went to bed 45 minutes early. The bright pink paper actually caught his attention and slowed him down a bit!"

for it on the weekends." Work with your needs and what you need to do, prioritizing when necessary.

How do you regroup? Some moms can take a power nap and grab twenty minutes when the kids nap or are in school. Even if you do not sleep, lying horizontal for twenty minutes helps boost your energy. The quietness soothes jangled nerves and revives your spirit. Katia, a stay-at-home mother of two, says, "Sometimes I feel like I am on my feet all day." She is up early with the kids and exhausted by the end of the day when her husband comes home from work. "A power nap saves me." She protects the time, and then has the stamina and energy for the second shift—the time when her husband gets home.

Our biological clocks follow individual patterns, and we can learn to recognize them. Maybe you have a daily low point, like this reader of my column:

Dear Genevieve,

What do you do if your own energy dip is at 3:30 in the afternoon (always been that way), which is just the time the kids are coming home tired and grumpy from school, and that's when their energy is low, too? How do you avoid meltdowns for everybody?

Signed,
Dippin' and Dazed
Palo Alto

Dear Dippin' and Dazed,

First assess your initial expectations or goals. The first part of success is defining what success is. Do you want to just get through a half hour without anyone bickering, or do you need to get everyone recharged for the next activity or homework assignment?

The midafternoon dip is notorious, and many people contend with a bit of low blood sugar or lack of energy. It sounds like you need to plan ahead or "train" for your energy dips. You are aware of a pattern, which is helpful, and now you can move to a solution.

Many moms swear that a bit of protein or fuel powers them and the kids though the midafternoon slump. They keep non-perishables such as nuts, powerbars, crackers and cheese or protein shakes handy in the car so that they can take "waterbreaks" wherever they are in the course of the daily mom marathon. Other moms try to arrive early somewhere and close their eyes for 5 minutes before the pickup. Still others find that the afternoon latte, tea, soda, or glass of icy cold water does the trick.

Rodney Aley, a well-known physical fitness instructor and personal trainer in Palo Alto, suggests some quick push-ups, sit-ups, or chest presses to "wake up the body." He also recommends a vitamin drink boost such as "Emer'gen-C," which you can find at local heath food stores such as Whole Foods and Trader Joe's, to contend with the daily slump.

A family pickup? How about a short walk, scooter ride, or bit of basketball to get some fresh air before settling down to do homework? If you pick up the intensity, you will feel more energized. Or put on some fun music with little ones and dance around the house.

Another approach? Aromatherapy can also boost your spirits. Keep some refreshing lemon, vanilla, mint, or another favorite scented lotion in your car or purse. Close your eyes, take a deep breath, say an affirmation or something positive to think about, and you can be on your way. One mom even uses glitter lotion for her girls and gives them a bit of "magic dust" to change the mood.

If you are particularly weary or your patience tank is running on empty, give your kids the heads-up. By letting them in on your limits, you are teaching them healthy coping skills.

Sincerely,
Genevieve

Maybe you cannot squeeze a nap in, but sitting for five minutes with a cup of coffee, Green Tea, or glass of cold lemonade recharges and refreshes you. How about using paper plates for dinner, getting take-out, or meeting another friend and her kids for a picnic in the park to lighten the load and your mood? Want some more ideas? Go back to Chapter 6: Pacing and Endurance for Moms for more ways to recharge.

🚩 Red Flag: Packing Too Much In

The end of a long, busy day can be full of risk for hitting the wall. Sometimes it helps to look back at a day, after things have become calm and quiet, and ask yourself how you could have changed it for the better. At the end of a bumpy day, just sit down and cast your mind back. Rethink your pacing. How can you improve your pace throughout the day so that you have more energy for the final stretch? You can cram a day full of busy activity, zoom from one commitment to another, but if you lose it in the late afternoon over something little, or if your children go into an exhausted meltdown, it's time to ask yourself, "Was it all worth it?"

Linda notes: "I know I have hit the wall when I am trying to do too many things in one day and then I am tired from it. If I think through all that I want to accomplish, say in a week's time, I can pace myself. Something I initially think I am going to get done on one day, if I take time to think about it, can actually happen the next day and life will still go on." Minako recalls that "when I get emotional or irritated easily, that's the point I need to slow down a little bit."

Mom Story

Dierdra knows that she is hitting a wall when "things are sliding in all different areas of my life. I have stacks of grading, I haven't spent one-to-one time lately with my child." Other clues for her: "Running late to everything, exhaustion level, not relating in a positive way to people I love, just asking them the more functional questions. I become much less available and open." She then knows she needs to "start going to bed earlier, let some things slide. Big one for me is letting go of expectations." Her house may not be spotless but it is comfortable. "When others come over, rather than feel embarrassed, I realize that their kids can play with the toys in the living room, and we can have some conversation time. Everyone is relaxed. It's great." Letting go of dated or unrealistic expectations is a key to pacing.

Mom Tip

Perhaps some items on the agenda really are not urgent. Perhaps one outing a day is really all your three-year-old can handle. Maybe you need to turn down a party or dinner invitation on the weekend to help both you and your family get grounded and reconnect, especially if you have older kids.

Slow down. Change the pace. By editing your schedule or your family's schedule, you can change your day, your outlook, and your energy. Need more ideas about ways to slow down and edit? Go back to Chapter 5: Mom Training Tips and Tools.

Red Flag: Can't Do It All

Sometimes fatigue sneaks up on you a little bit at a time. You aren't overwhelmed on any given day, but you may have been feeling stretched thin for a while. When you hit the wall because of this kind of stealth fatigue, it can be hard to figure out why it happened. Then you want to take a look at your priorities and make some changes. Perhaps you are in a particularly demanding phase of child rearing or find yourself in a dynamic that is not what you want. Annie, a stay-at-home mother of three, says, "I don't have the energy for all of it. My relationship with my husband is suffering somewhat, dormant. I need to spend more time with my husband. Go on more walks together." Annie is not hitting the wall because of this, but her unhappiness with the status quo could wear her down, sapping her mood and energy. Prioritization tools such as you find in Chapter 2 can always be a boon.

Sometimes the wall is triggered by guilt: You're getting lots of things done, but not the thing that most needs doing and you feel guilty about it. Maybe your marriage needs some attention. Cancel some plans to add a date night. Better yet, set up a weekly date night. You don't even have to leave the house. After the kids are in bed or the teens in their rooms, order takeout and eat on your nice dishes. Throw in some candles. Pretend you are in a restaurant—and you don't even have to pay a sitter.

Enrichment activities for kids can be wonderful, and hard to resist. Adopt some guidelines to prevent over committing to them. When you are too tightly scheduled, you can experience a constant, low-level fatigue.

Dear Genevieve,

I have been listening to moms for many years now. Most of them talk about how hard it is to balance life with the many schedules/activities we receive as parents. My mom told me several years ago that "you will eventually do what all your other sisters before you have done. Slow it down." I thought, why wait? Why not learn from my sisters and mom now instead of learning the hard way? So I decided to set limits on the number of extracurricular activities I offer my kids. I came up with 'no double-bookings,' meaning no activities that overlap (i.e., soccer season with basketball season).

Recently my husband has started signing up the kids, first with basketball. So I postponed my daughters' gymnastics until after basketball season. Then came softball, which overlaps with the swim team. I don't care if my kids do both, just not at the same time. Like maybe softball one year and swimming the next. Or cut softball out early to start swimming. My husband strongly feels that sports are crucial to growing up. I even agree with him but with limits, so I decided to adjust the "no double-booking rule" to apply only during the school year and open it up during the summer. I feel too many sports cut into our family time (because surely they don't cut into laundry time, paying bills time or grocery shopping time). Any advice?

Signed,
Double Trouble
Palo Alto, CA

Dear Double Trouble,

Your concerns are common among families today. How do we give our kids varied opportunities but not at the expense of family time? As the kids get older it can be harder to set limits, because kids are specializing earlier and team seasons can spill over into preseason or year-round practices.

Now is a great time to sit down with your husband and focus on your home team and dynamic. If he and the kids want multiple sports, maybe you can have an activity limit per week. If practices fall on the same days for two different sports, pick only one to go to, even if you could physically make it to two.

I recently interviewed someone whose family has decided that homework has to be completed before participating in activities or sports. Sometimes this means their child has to be late to his baseball game in order to make sure his work is done.

What is the tone in your home? You get to set the pace, taking into account your own family's need and dynamics. Be sure to schedule some family down time or "water breaks" on your calendar. In your case, this could mean getting the whole family involved in a sport such as hiking, tennis, boating, surfing, swimming, skiing, etc. A Saturday to the beach or mountains may mean missing a game, but it will be worth it in the long run.

Sincerely,

Genevieve

Red Flag: Tantrums

When a child has a tantrum, that kid has hit the wall. Something in his or her development or day or diet, or all of the above, has pushed the child too far. And because little kids have so few tools to deal with their emotions, they sometimes just lose it! Having to deal with a tantrum can be more physically and emotionally exhausting than a root canal, but the last thing you want is to get caught up in the tantrum's emotional force field and hit the wall, too. When training for tantrums, you have to watch for your kid's red flags and your own, too. You know your child's patterns better than anyone else: try not to put your child in a situation where a tantrum is likely. Having done that, if you miss the signals or if a tantrum just comes out of the blue, don't let it send you crashing into a wall, too. Have a plan to deal with tantrums and their aftermath.

Do you ever feel helpless after contending with a tantrum? Or feel embarrassed by the public spectacle? Some days are simply more challenging than others. I am always amazed by the intensity that my children have as they move in and out of phases of development. The Terrific Twos (also known as the Terrible Twos) are both comical and taxing. They are usually taxing at the time and comical in the retelling. You can know (and believe!) that a two-year-old's fierce independence is important to developing self-reliance yet still wonder where your child came from—another planet perhaps?

When I feel particularly challenged, I like to reframe my day as an adventure or a ride. I find it particularly helpful to know that we can always start over. This is such a useful tool! It's available anytime, anywhere. For example, if I sense that things are going in the wrong direction, if the kids are squabbling for no good reason, if one of my kids is recovering from a tantrum, we stop and I ask everybody to start the day over. My children are not only learning to start their day over, but they love the feeling that they can have a new beginning. You can feel their relief! Suddenly, they don't have to finish that silly argument they got stuck in. Sometimes, I even need to start *my* day over so that I can find more patience and a fresh perspective. We have been known to start our day over five times until we get it right. Ten times would be okay; there's no limit on start overs! (See Appendix B: Tantrum Strategies from Moms in the Trenches.)

RED FLAG! Red Flag: Worry

To be a mother means to worry—somewhat. You can worry about your kids, your marriage, your job, or terrorism. There is always plenty to worry about. Worry can sap your energy like nothing else. A little worry is normal, but for some moms worry becomes debilitating.

If you are anxious about every accident your child could possibly have, you might need to let go a little bit. You cannot control life. You can make some things easier and parent with caution, but you don't need to have your children wear bubble suits during flu season to keep them from getting sick.

With infants and toddlers, you do have to be on your toes or they will chew on a lamp cord, find a button or Lego on the ground and swallow it, put their fingers in a door hinge, go headfirst into the tub, or drink from the toilet. Suzanne notes that "all of that 'psychic awareness,' also known as the danger radar, drains your energy and wipes you out."

Worry exhausts you, so what can you do about it? Chandra, a mother of two teenagers, realized one day "that I spent too much time and energy thinking of all the ways the boys could hurt themselves and preventing the possible accidents." So she decided to "change my outlook and not be so fearful. I am happier and the kids are more at ease! Kids pick up on the worry and can become very fearful. I didn't want that!" Sometimes you just have to let go a little bit. You cannot control your child's every move in order to protect him or her. They learn from their mistakes and their skinned knees. If you insulate them from every harm, how are they are ever going to learn to trust their own judgment when they enter the real world?

A few years ago, I found that I was worrying too much about a job transition, a possible relocation, and a couple of friends who were going through life crises. These very real concerns began to weigh heavily on me. By sharing my fears with my support network, specifically my prayer group, I began to lighten my load. I also picked a running race to train for to distract me, and I began writing each night, earnestly working on a new manuscript. My accountability buddies and support networks eased my fears, the exercise burned up the anxious feelings, and the writing served to fuel my inner passions. Many good things came from facing up to my worries.

Red Flag: Down Days and Depression

The media has made us more aware of what happens to mothers if they hit the wall. We hear all kinds of stories about mothers struggling with postpartum depression, from those who kill their children to celebrities like Brooke Shields who talk about it and get the help they need. Although everyone hits a wall now and then, you don't have to hit a wall hard. Mothers today can find the support they need if they know where to look and if their support network helps them detect the early warning signs. Those mothers can identify red flags and triggers early and prevent themselves from hitting a wall, or at least slow the impact so they can cope with the aftermath. There are so many resources and strategies available that can be tailored to the ups and downs of mothering, such as www.postpartum.net, which is the Postpartum Support International's website, or Shoshanna S. Bennett and Pec

Indman's book *Beyond the Blues: A Guide to Understanding and Treating Prenatal and Postpartum Depression.*

We can all have our down days. They happen for many reasons: lack of sleep, hormones, relationship problems, or the weather. But what do you do about these down days? Katia realizes that "when I go down, I hurt people—myself and my family." She finds that the arts restore her and energize her. Her salsa class is "really a kick. I sweat and let it all out. I'm lousy. I don't care. I am learning a lot about my body." She loves her work, which also serves to balance out her mothering. "If I didn't do my own thing, I would overwhelm the kids. I would drive them nuts giving them idea after idea, living through them." For more about restorative tools, go back to Chapter 6: Pacing and Endurance for Moms.

> **Mom Story**
>
> Katia also uses different kinds of music to boost her mood. "Every time I feel a little depressed, I go for Chopin or I try to do the opposite and get Habib Koite for balance!"

Sonia recognizes and accepts her patterns and has her stash of strategies. "I have set days to watch out for and prescribed antidotes." Rainy and foul weather days, for instance, "always make me cranky." So she and the kids, "call these 'buzzy days,' and we play games and have hot chocolate and light a fire in the fireplace." On "winter days, we take walks outside. On long days, we all take baths together in the hot tub or, when the kids were small, in the bathtub. If someone is sick, we rent a movie (otherwise we don't watch much TV). We allow computer game time during the cranky hour only."

Be gentle with yourself. Rubie, a stay-at-home mother of two, takes a "time out on an issue" when necessary. "I have to be able to tell myself that the issue is creating too much stress to resolve now, and I will return to it when I am not stressed. Sometimes it takes research like reading, a class on the topic or a specialist in the area." Sometimes you need to outsource or take a break in order to gain some clarity and move through or around a stumbling block.

🚩 Red Flag: In a Rut

Perhaps your version of hitting the wall feels more like being in a rut. You have no desire to put one foot in front of the other. You are cooked. You are toast. Enthusiasm feels like a bad word. When you hit the fitness center, all you can think about is getting to the shower afterwards.

Do something about it. Keep experimenting until you find what works. Change things a bit. If you are running, change the pace. Change the scenery. Hit more trails, parks, and new terrain. In your life, try going to bed earlier and getting up earlier to give yourself some fresh alone time in the early morning. Sign up for a low-cost class through a local community center. Take up hula, belly, or tap dancing. Change the intensity of something you are doing. Throw in steps or stadiums. Add speed work. If you work out at the gym, vary the machines. Try new ones. Find out about kickboxing, spinning, yoga, and Tae Kwon Do.

A sense of progress can really fire up your engines. If you are working towards a new goal, add a few more hours a week to feel the energy boost provided by new progress. The sense of accomplishment will fuel you through your week. Looking for team players and support? Try basketball games at the local YMCA, ultimate Frisbee, volleyball, tennis, squash, racquetball, or golf. Join a running, hiking, or swimming club. Go rollerblading. Try to find a family exercise activity that all can enjoy.

Put a notice up at your local school, library, YMCA, or community bulletin board to find someone else who might share your interest, whether it be walking on trails or beginning a band. Accountability buddies and support networks can push you past your self-imposed roadblocks. **Just keep moving.** You can do it.

In a rut with writing, painting, drawing, researching? Try another approach, another perspective, another topic. Remember, going sideways can also be progress. One time, when I was suffering writer's block with *The Sport of Motherhood* and felt frustrated, inarticulate and self-critical, I switched to researching more and focusing on the end-of-the-chapter exercises. As I made progress, I began to feel like I was accomplishing something. I was excited and reenergized. When I was ready to switch back to the writing, I realized how much progress that I had actually made in other areas of my project! The new ideas and direction had given me a break from the writing, but had also fueled me up with new ideas and resources. I had kept moving. When I circled back to the trouble spot, it was gone.

> **Mom Story**
>
> "My first job selling copiers was MISERABLE. My mother gave me a good tip when I was having a hard time getting started. She would often start by doing a load of laundry and getting some energy going and then build the confidence to make the difficult phone calls while achieving one of the things on her list. So, I would start with the easy things on my list and get the confidence to tackle the difficult. I am different now. I tackle the difficult things first to get them done so that I might have some peace in my busy head." —Elise

In a rut with the kids? Spice things up a bit. Try new places and new playgrounds. Make an effort to connect with different moms. Designate one day a week to be Adventure Day. On this day, you and the kids try something new, whether it's a new playground, a new train museum, a hike, a trip to a new town. Just keep moving.

When we moved to San Francisco with my two-year-old and three-month-old, we knew just a handful of people. I decided to implement my Adventure Day strategy to check out new places, have some fun, and get to know other moms in the process. I trolled the playgrounds, asking other moms their favorite places to go with their kids, and got some great ideas that way. I consulted resource books on places to go with kids, and I also just explored.

Wednesdays became Adventure Day. People that met me soon found out that I did this on Wednesdays and learned that they could join me or not. I got to know the Bay Area well and connected with other moms and kids in the process.

Create your own version of Adventure Day. Try it. Do it. When you are in a rut, change the scenery and keep moving. You can regain your stride and your enthusiasm.

🚩 Red Flag: Loneliness

You can be lonely in the middle of a crowd or with a pack of kids. So often, mothers need time to connect with adults. Working mothers have an easier time of this since they typically enjoy adult interaction and feedback at their jobs; however, the many mothers who work out of the home can feel isolated and disconnected. In fact, one of my email exchanges with a friend offers a typical scenario. I had recently upped my work hours on *The Sport of Motherhood* and was feeling the change. I emailed a peer, who has been working from home for a long time, to hear her take on things:

> "Do you ever feel kind of alone as you manage your work hours? Just wondering. Maybe I just feel that way at times because my unpaid 'work' is solitary." (Me)
>
> "About the work—Yes, I definitely feel alone, and sometimes lonely, when I'm mapping out the work/deadlines and actually doing it. This kind of work is only partly a good fit for me—it is best when I can combine it with some collaboration and just goofing-off time with colleagues. That's what I miss most about not being in a 'regular job.' However, I don't miss the politics, the rigid schedule, etc., etc., so I'm gradually learning ways to cope with the solitariness. I really like some of the alone time, but not all of it! We should talk! :-)" (Suzanne)

Loneliness can crop up unexpectedly but some situations, such as the birth of a first child, relocation, or a new job, are known to trigger bouts of loneliness. With the birth of the first child, the new mother needs to meet other moms of newborns. You can do this through local hospitals and mothers' groups or even national mothers' groups. Many national groups, such as La Leche League and Las Madres, can help you find local chapters. Get connected. Get support. Suzanne found "email was a lifeline and still is—and getting on the phone." Chat rooms, blogs, and resources found on sites such as www.clubmom.com, www.BlueSuitMom.com, www.siliconmom.com, www.svmomblog.com, and www.mothersclick.com offer a variety of topics and ways to connect. For more info and how-to suggestions, go to Chapter 4: Building a Personalized Support Network.

Job relocation affects the entire family. Not only do you need to get your family resettled with schools, doctors, and other necessary services, you also have to help your kids and yourself settle in, get the lay of the land, and connect with new people.

What do you do when you feel lonely or disconnected? Do you stay silent and bear it or reach out to a friend or fellow mom? Do you isolate yourself because you lack the energy to be around others, or do you get up and out of the house? Do something about loneliness. Join a book group, a playgroup, or hang out at Starbuck's one morning a week with a friend. If your situation makes you lonely, find a way to change it. Don't know what to do? Ask your friends, your mom, a spiritual being, or tell your dog about it. Give someone a hug.

Sometimes you need to rediscover the people in your own home. It can be lonely being on different schedules from our loved ones. Here's a letter I received from a woman who just didn't see enough of her husband:

Dear Genevieve,

Dad is up and out of the house by 6:00 a.m. Mom is in bed by 8:30. How do we find time to connect?

Signed,

Exhausted and Lonely

Palo Alto, CA

Dear Exhausted and Lonely,

You and your husband are currently on different race courses. How can you meet in the middle? Sounds like you two need to sit down and come up with some strategies together. He has to leave by 6 a.m. So you need to work with that fact.

You can try going to bed a bit later with the understanding that you get some focused "date time" or "just the two of you time" before bed. One way to recharge, since this is your usual bedtime, is to take a shower or bath and wash the kid-day off of you. It can help you take off your mom hat and put on your "wife" or "interesting individual" hat! Meet in the living room with a cup of hot chocolate or a glass of lemon water. You can talk, play cards or a board game, or even watch a movie now and then. The focused time together will give you the boost you want.

You can also flip it around and both get up a bit earlier when you are fresh. Have a leisurely breakfast together in the wee hours before the kids get up. You may be a little more tired at first, but in a week or two, you will soon find your stride.

Sincerely,

Genevieve

Red Flag: Resentments

Resentments are toxic. It is important to identify them and do something about them. With enough awareness, you may be able to recognize triggers early on and thus prevent resentment! Sonia notes: "When I become aware of a resentment, I realize it is time to adjust my life. When I find the power to change my life, I feel better. The resentment comes from my perception that I am powerless and trapped. The antidote is to make a small change that says I'm not. For instance, if I resent the times my husband is away on business, it usually is because he is doing something new and interesting or because of the free time he has at night to watch any movie he wants."

When she recognizes why she is resentful towards her husband, she addresses it. "I need to get out and do something new and interesting. One time I took a trip to see an old friend with the kids, but another time I made a deal with my husband that before he went away, I got a day off to go somewhere myself. For me, it's not that I need equal away time, but I need to feel I have the power to have the same time—then I'm happy."

Miya, a working mom of one, tries to "save up 'notes' in my head to my husband and talk to him during a quiet time, instead of nagging or snapping in the heat of the moment. He hears it better then, and I deliver it better. With the baby, I try desperately to take a deep breath when she does something 'not okay'—like hitting. I constantly try to read baby books and parenting magazines to get fresh perspectives and reminders. I find this really helpful with a toddler—I can see 'that's why she's doing that'—and it makes sense to me and helps me deal with the behavior in a better way."

> **Mom Story**
>
> Robbie, a mother of two, calls herself "a hybrid: a stay-at-home mom who is starting her own home-based business and considering doing a bit of part-time work just to get out of the house, have some adult interaction and maybe even get back a feeling of autonomy." She finds that resentments "come from not feeling appreciated for all the hard work I do as 'just a mom.'" She uses mantras to change her attitude. "My main one now is 'Don't take it personally.' I also say a little daily prayer, which asks God to guide my thinking and my actions and to give me some self-esteem." (For more about mantras and affirmations, see Chapter 6: Pacing and Endurance for Moms.)

Stay-at-home mothers can feel a loss of autonomy or identity. Adrienne, a mother of two, exclaims, "It is always my fault when we run out of money. I do not have any financial independence, which would be nice. I do everything for everyone in my house, and I am raising boys. This bothers me." To address her feelings, she "pray[s] at night for thanks and my blessings. I try not to go to bed mad." She also now has her boys helping with a few chores around the house, which eases her load and her mind.

Dierdra has become wiser with age in the way she handles resentments. She has learned "there is not going to be a positive outcome if I wait until I am so angry and only able to talk about it in a negative way. They won't hear me. I am working on being more forthright and voicing things right away. Some toxic people you can't get away from, like at work, and I have trouble dealing with them on the spot." Over time, though, she watches "how others do it, read about how to do it, practice," and it gets easier. She has learned to "identify the problem" that is bothering her.

Deidre learned another key concept: "I can only change how I react to a certain situation or a person. I can't change them." Prayers and advice books can help you to cope. The twelve-step Serenity Prayer (written by American theologian Reinhold Niebuhr: "God grant me the Serenity to accept the things I cannot change, the Courage to change the things I can, and the Wisdom to know the difference.") is a soothing balm, and Richard Carlson's book *Don't Sweat the Small Stuff with Your Family: Simple Ways to Keep Daily Responsibilities and Household Chaos from Taking Over Your Life* provides wonderful ideas for defeating resentment.

Lana says she and her husband "work well together when it comes to parenting. The last thing we want to do is be ambiguous. Resentments usually emerge about extended family (in-laws mostly) and what they expect of us. We have learned to talk about things and assert ourselves. We try not to hold onto our resentments, because all that does is make us tired!"

Talk it out. When you let resentments build up, you can explode over something little. Is that what you want? If talking it over with the offending party does not work, many moms talk it out to a sympathetic ear or pray to let go. Write a letter you would never send or write in your journal. Use your imagination. A friend once told me that she liked to hold imaginary dinner parties for the hurtful people she was angry with. They had to eat with each other at her table, suffering each other's company. By the way, no dessert! After that, her resentments were gone.

Red Flag: Jealousy and Insecurity

When jealousy crops up, you are more likely than not comparing your insides to another's outside. You don't know the full story behind the other person. Feelings of jealousy often flare up out of self-doubt. Rather than dwelling on your faults or have-nots, affirm what you have and who you are. You can also do some footwork and make some changes.

When Dierdra doubts herself, she "tries to use positive language" and affirm what she is trying to do. Marisa, a mom of two, says she gets "jealous of my husband's activities, like being in a band, drumming, singing, acting, writing, gardening, connecting with kids and making a difference in their lives, swimming, etc. To deal with this, I tell him how I feel, and he encourages me to jump in and do my own things like play tennis and grow my own business." She has been getting out more and working from home and loving it. Identifying the triggers and doing something about them is one way to curb jealousy.

I went to a Women's Symposium a few years ago and was bothered by the audience reaction to the concept of the "Perfect Mom." We were told to close our eyes and think of a perfect mom. Then we opened our eyes and the speaker had people call out their answers. As women in the symposium named different characteristics of their perfect mom, people began tearing "the Perfect Mom" down. One comment was, "She is good with arts and crafts with the kids, BUT SHE HAS A BRITTLE SMILE." What

I couldn't get over was that people weren't thinking of this perfect mom's whole story. We don't know what the rest of her life is like! Isn't this kind of thinking what we are teaching our children not to do?

How did we ever get to comparing ourselves against other moms? If a mom is good with arts and crafts, science projects, or math games, hooray for her! Let's be happy that she gets to enjoy doing this with her kids and their friends—can my kids enjoy the projects and games, too?

The word mother, by definition, describes a woman and her child. A mother isn't defined in comparison to other women or other moms. Let's celebrate and troubleshoot as needed as we raise our children to the best of our collective abilities. As I climb off my soapbox, let me state it succinctly: be gentle with yourself. Use positive language about yourself and other moms. Enjoy and benefit from the varied strengths of mothers around you.

Red Flag: Feelings of Failure

As we raise our kids to the best of our abilities, we also have to remember that each child is unique and has his or her own temperament and disposition. Though we may be able to instill some of our values and priorities, we cannot control how our children turn out.

Successful parenting is about letting our children go once we have given them the right values and skills to live their lives. When they make mistakes or the going gets tough, it may be hard not to blame ourselves and ask, "Where did I go wrong? How come my teenager thinks it is okay to talk to me this way?"

Tina captures this concern: "I have had a lot of trouble dealing with the 'terrible twos.' There were a few days when I thought, 'Where did I go wrong?' or 'There has to be something wrong with him' or 'There must be some kind of medication for this.' In talking with other parents, I found

> ### Mom Story
>
> "I do feel like I have failed at times, especially when I completely lose patience with them. This has always just been in my feelings, though. There are times when I would love to just walk out the door and leave them home to fend for themselves, but I never would. I often tell my husband, 'Tomorrow night I am getting a hotel room by myself to just sleep.' It helps me to talk about it, to imagine it, and then I feel better." —Tanya

that my kid was no more cranky or aggressive than any other two-year-old. Although it doesn't help much while he's throwing a huge fit, it makes me feel better knowing that I'm not alone."

Samia, a working mother of two, feels challenged getting one of her children motivated to do homework and do it well. "We hit a wall and try something new. It is hard not to feel like a failure when I don't know what to do, what will work for my daughter." She and her husband talk about different strategies and try them. They get on the same page and support each other along the way. New school years, new teachers, and new teaching styles present them with new challenges.

Keiko, a mom of three who has both worked full time and stayed at home, grapples with a mother's feelings of guilt and failure. When she feels guilty about accepting or wanting help from her mom, who lives nearby, she asks herself, "What's up with that? Is it about PRIDE? Just because I am not working full time doesn't mean I can't have some help. It used to take a village to raise a child but now, with everyone moving around for jobs and fear of kids being stolen out of the streets or molested by strangers, mothers are more isolated." The village is gone and it is up to the mom, typically, to make up for it.

Keiko concludes: "I need to talk to others to gain perspective because I am not very objective with myself. I certainly don't hold others up to my standards." She likes to "get rid of the shoulds. Shoulds sap your energy and are a waste of time."

Parents raising teenagers can tell us a lot about dreading failure. Teenagers grow bigger than you, but they still need to abide by your house rules. Viviana says, "I have raised a very nice boy, but sometimes he thinks he is big enough to make all his decisions. But he is not; he still has to follow my rules." For example, "I don't want girls calling the house in the middle of the night. So now I set up a phone time for him. From 7 to 9 p.m. he can talk on the phone. I didn't send him to school to find a girlfriend. Teenagers can be hard. Sometimes you feel like a failure. How do you know what to do sometimes? My husband and I, we try our best."

When you are depressed, everything takes on a different, gloomy hue. Some moms I interviewed equated depression with a "feeling of failure." Rubie, a stay-at-home mother of two, points out that sometimes you need "a specialist to slowly teach you what it means when you are depressed. Allow yourself recognition of where you are and set small steps to a goal and fulfill it."

> **MOM TIP**
>
> "Stop 'shoulding' on yourself. Don't say, 'I should be able to do x, y, or z.' Say 'I can do it!' Affirm what you are able to do."
> —Val

Sometimes depression is situational and you can handle it on your own, but if you feel like doom and gloom for too long, maybe you need some professional support.

Are You Stuck?

Do you feel blocked or stuck? You feel like you can't put in the time towards your goal because of kids, shopping, and the PTA. Or was that the in-laws, soup, and broken plumbing? Whatever your reasons, regroup. Go to the "Strategic Plan Table" in Chapter 2 and go back through the exercise. It is easy and can enlighten you. Note your objective. What is your obstacle? Who are you allies and resources? What is the next step for you to help you work towards your goal?

> **MOM TIP**
>
> Fear can slow you down or even cripple you. Part of the problem is that many people are afraid to take a risk and lose. What if you look at it a different way? If you take a risk and try something, you are actually moving forward. If you do not succeed in your first attempt or don't produce work of the caliber you wanted, at least you have tried. You don't have to be finished after that first attempt. You can learn and go on!

How can you make progress if you don't get messy and give something a good try? Maybe you make a new decision on the other side of your attempt. At least it is a more informed decision. If you make a mistake, you learned from it. You will have new information the next time you are in the same situation. Don't be afraid to get messy, to get real.

Take a few minutes and write down what is blocking you from your goal. What are you afraid of? Are you worried what others will think? Are you worried about life changing on you? By acknowledging your fear, you create awareness. With awareness comes discomfort. With discomfort comes change and newfound clarity.

More on Coping Strategies and Tools

1. Time-Outs—For YOU!

Okay, so you know how to give a child a time-out to help him or her regroup. What about you? How do you give yourself a time-out? Practice giving yourself a time-out when you need it. Make sure that any younger children are safe (put one in a crib, if necessary), then walk out of the room and take a deep breath.

Sometimes a mom's time-out looks a lot like a prayer or a hobby. Some moms like to use daily Affirmations or Meditations geared towards mothers, women who do too much, recovery programs, or their faith. Others find solace in the bathroom, garage, or garden. Carlita, a stay-at-home mom of two, tells me that "when the kids were little, sometimes I put them to bed early, would take a monitor outside and garden until dark."

2. Escape Fantasies

Believe it or not, you are not alone in this. Most mothers have momentary escape fantasies. They can range from dreaming about a past or future life to a loud voice in your head screaming, "Help! Get me out of the kitchen and into a cozy bed!" You may just yearn to go meet some adult friends or go to a movie on a whim without having to work out childcare arrangements.

It's normal. Accept your feelings for what they are. Call a friend. Try

> **Mom Story**
>
> After the birth of my third child, I had a primal urge to escape and found myself in the tub up to three times a day for self-preservation. I was operating instinctively on a need for personal space. The older two children would come to the tub and peer over, asking to get in. "Nope, only mommy's bath this time," I would say.

to laugh and keep plugging away. You can't get out of this mom marathon, but you can reassess and adapt. Do you need to slow everyone's schedule down? Maybe afternoon activities for the older sibling do not work for the younger one. If the younger is throwing tantrums after an afternoon nap every day because she is still tired, connect the dots. She may really need more down time.

3. (Re)Gaining Perspective: Sayings

Bring out your Attitude Toolkit from Chapter 6: Pacing and Endurance for Moms. Attitude is key to reframing your mood and your day. If you can open yourself up to the brighter side of things, you can enjoy the journey instead of focusing on the outcome or your expectations.

Several moms I interviewed have found perspective by taking a long view on the whole mom. Dana, a stay-at-home mother of two, views her life through the long lens: "Women live lives in chapters." She realizes that she does not have to do it all at the same time. She has a whole life to live.

But how do you gain perspective in the mothering moment? Chris reminds herself when "the kids are being kids in overdrive" that "I asked for this!" When my daughter is talking a red streak and I can't listen anymore, I tell try to tell myself, "You taught her how to talk and delighted in those first words and phrases. NOW OPEN YOU EARS AND HEART AND LISTEN TO AND BE IN AWE OF HER AS YOU DID BACK THEN!!!"

4. Parenting Books and Educational Resources

You can use the Internet on your own or Amazon's rating and critique list. According to Margaret, a working mom of two, it makes sense to "read books to get ideas on how to handle" new situations or troubleshoot as needed. No need to live in a vacuum.

Librarians can be particularly helpful if you are seeking age-appropriate books for your child to read on topics ranging

> **Mom Story**
>
> Jackie, a working mom of two who raised one of her children by herself for a number of years, has a good attitude: "I just keep telling myself, I have to give up what I expected in life in order to make myself open to what is meant for me. . . which could be something really great . . . something I cannot even imagine yet."

from new siblings, peer pressure, bullying, cliques, death, divorce, or long-term illness. American Girl has helpful and accessible books for kids such as *The Feelings Book: The Care and Keeping of your Emotions* by Norm Bendell and Lynda Madison and *The Care and Keeping of You: The Body Book for Girls* by Valorie Schaefer and Norm Bendell, as well as books on topics like dealing with divorce. Of course for younger kids, the Berenstain Bears series by Stan and Jan Berenstain addresses a range of handy topics from teasing to handling strangers to keeping toys picked up to eating too much junk food. Ask your pediatrician or mothers' group for tips. Check out the lecture series or discussion groups at your local parenting community center.

Wrap-Up

Moms can hit three kinds of walls: life-changing, situational, and seasonal. In this chapter, we focused primarily on the latter two. Whether a wall arises because of exhaustion, loneliness, the terrible twos, or teenage black clouds, there are ways to get beyond it. Just like a marathon runner, a mom can to train for the wall.

Increased awareness of the phenomena allows you to effectively use your resources. Just as we are all different, we also may need different tools for similar situations. You can customize your training. The key is to try the tools until you find what works. Using trial and error, hone in on what works best for you and your specific situation. If a tool doesn't *quite* work for you, make an adjustment in how you use it. If a tool doesn't work for you *at all*, set it aside and try another. Support networks or perhaps professional help can help you go the distance. Remember, parenthood is not a competitive sport but an endurance sport. If we pool our resources and troubleshoot together, we can bounce back from many of the walls that we hit along the way and more fully enjoy the course of the day.

Now let's go on to life-changing walls that feel like you are being hit by a truck.

EXERCISES

Warm Up: Reflective Stretches

1. When you hit a wall or are faced with a challenging situation, do you (circle the answers that apply to you):

    - bark at the next person on your path? **Yes or No**
    - take a deep breath? **Yes or No**
    - reach out and call someone? **Yes or No**
    - hole up in your room and draw the blinds? **Yes or No**
    - write in a journal? **Yes or No**
    - pray? **Yes or No**
    - feel paralyzed? **Yes or No**
    - begin to gather information via web, research, etc.? **Yes or No**
    - go it alone because you don't want to lean on anyone or look weak? **Yes or No**
    - put a priority on getting enough sleep and eating well? **Yes or No**
    - name what you are feeling? **Yes or No**

    Look at your answers. What do YOU tend to do?

2. Name three situations that can challenge your peace of mind (examples: large family gatherings, computer problems, work or volunteer deadlines, children's meltdowns, plans going awry, chaotic situations, sibling fights, car or house problems, bill-paying, leaky roof, etc.).

    a. _____
    b. _____
    c. _____

3. Can you identify any triggers or red flags preceding those walls (examples: fatigue, poor health, guilt, no personal time, no family time, isolation, overscheduled, 3 o'clock slump, etc.)?

    a. _____

    b. _____

Practice: Coping Skills Toolbox

1. List two ways that you can take a "time out" or get some much-needed personal time.

       a. _____

       b. _____

2. When you are in a rut, what are some ways to get "unstuck"? (ruts might include: don't want to exercise or eat well; not motivated to do work; feel blah; are only going through the motions; etc.).

       a. _____

       b. _____

       c. _____

3. Get realistic: what are some balls you can drop?

       a. _____

       b. _____

Complete an ATTITUDE TOOLKIT

Here is an example format for an Attitude Toolkit. Go to Chapter 6 if you need more details.

Perspective	Name two ways to help someone without them knowing it.	1. 2.
Affirmations	Write down a couple of short (three-word) affirmations tailored to your interests or needs.	1. 2. 3.
Daily Readings	What type of daily reading could boost your spirits? (inspiration, meditation, quote of day?)	1. 2. 3.
Humor	List three examples of where you can find humor and/or people who make you smile/laugh.	1. 2.
Gratitude Checklist	Name two things for which you can be thankful.	1. 2.

Cool-Down

Write down one person who might recognize some of your common walls, red flags, or patterns.

_____

CHAPTER 8

Being Hit by a Truck

> ▶ R U feeling paralyzed, depressed, or overwhelmed by a life-changing event?
> ▶ How about some tips, tools, + resources from other moms N the trenches?

We all know that family life brings difficulty and sorrow as well as joy, comfort, and pleasure. Some of us face enormous challenges. Everyone has her share of heartache. When you are facing such a time, you are facing a life-changing wall. It's hard to prepare for this; because these walls rise up with such force, hitting one feels like being hit by a truck. The impact on you and your life can be huge. There are two kinds of experiences that can hit us with the impact of a truck: events that happen at a single point in time and require healing, such as an accident or death, and unexpected burdens that change our lives forever, such as raising a special needs child, divorcing, or having cancer. Unfortunately, being in any of these situations, hitting any of these life-changing walls, also makes it more likely that we'll hit other, lesser walls as well. Living through an unexpected tragedy or burden means that you will draw on your training and inner resources in new ways.

When bad things happen, it helps to acknowledge what has happened and give yourself time to grieve in order to find solace and heal. In other words, slow the pace down by taking off nonessential to-do items. Grief can be messy and awkward. Grief can come at unexpected times; yet grief is a part of healing and an integral part of life. When we let our feelings come up, when we actually sit with them, we engage in the healing process and begin the real journey—where the past informs the present creating a new reality.

According to the bereaved parents and experts on *The Sport of Motherhood's* "Honoring Grief" TV Show, each person's grieving journey is unique. There is no "right way" to grieve. Men can grieve differently than women. For example, Carl Yorke, whose son died of cancer, does not want to be hugged, whereas Audrey Jacobs, who miscarried, does.

Liz Powell, Director of Kara's Youth and Family Service Program and whose brother committed suicide, mentions that it is important to not be afraid of different grieving styles and needs within a bereaved family. Some people may need to talk it out while others want to write about it or not talk about the loss at all. Some may seek support groups, professional help, or self-help books, while others may not. Some may need to nurture something such as a plant or new pet, while others may throw themselves into a creative or physical outlet.

At a certain point, people may find themselves heading towards what Liz calls, "The New Normal." Life will not go back to what it was, but there is a new future that incorporates the loss from the past with a bit of hope. A move can even sound fun again. At this point, Rev. Sally Brown, suggests picking up a recreational activity that peaks interest such as hiking or biking. To see the show *"Honoring Grief: The Real Journey," go to www.sportofmotherhood.com/TVShow.htm*.

Emotional turmoil or a heavy heart saps your energy and weighs you down. If possible, lighten your load. Remember, some things don't have to be done right then. They can wait, especially in the aftermath of a sudden event like this. Be gentle with yourself about living up to expectations in other areas of your life. I am not an expert in this particular field though I have experienced my own loss and grief, but I think it is important to touch briefly on the most common forms of this type of tragedy. During times of heavy crisis, support is critical, so review Chapter 4 for tips on support networks.

Accidents

Mothers spend so much time worrying about accidents for a good reason: kids don't know how to take care of themselves and accidents do happen. Balancing between reasonable and unreasonable fear is one of the most difficult aspects of raising children. How do you cope? Whom do you look to for support?

While raising my brood of four children, we have been faced with a couple of hair-raising accidents. Here is the story on one of them. In the summer of 2004, while my family and I were in a remote area of Wyoming at a dude ranch, we had a real scare with Lilly, who was 13 months old at the time. My husband Keen and I had each been hit with a 24-hour stomach bug the day before we returned home. We were too dizzy and ill to pack when the kids were asleep, and so we ended up packing the day of our departure.

As I was packing us up, going back and forth between two rooms, Lilly happily played with the folded laundry amidst all the other things that still needed to go into suitcases. I didn't think much of it since she was clearly entertained in the corner of the room, but while I packed, she got into a travel-size bottle of Advil that had a childproof cap.

Somehow she undid the cap and ate—chewed and swallowed—eight adult-dosage Advil tablets in a matter of minutes.

We didn't have cell service, so Keen ran up to the main cabin and called 911 and Poison Control while I made Lilly throw up by jamming my finger down her throat. Keen tore back to the cabin, and told me Poison Control wanted us to count the pills she threw up. We could only find the shells of perhaps four amidst some brightly colored goldfish crackers that she had just eaten. This meant she had at least four in her and had ingested the medicine of almost all of them.

We raced back up to the main house and the phone line. Lilly became lethargic pretty quickly. We gave her a cup of half-and-half—all that the ranch house had—to slow down the absorption while we waited. The ambulance took 30 minutes to get to us due to the remote location and bumpy ranch roads.

When the ambulance arrived, they took her vitals and gave her oxygen. She soon perked up and looked better, but we still did not know if her organs, specifically her kidneys, were going to be okay.

During all of this, I prayed to God: "Dear Lord, I know that our children are gifts from you, but to please don't take her away just yet. Please give us a little more time with her."

Afterwards, I was emotionally spent. I realized that I needed to be gentle with myself and eased up on my writing schedule. When I was ready, I wrote about the accident and emailed it to some friends, family, and the Assistant Rector at our church, seeking, perhaps, a dose of perspective and closure. I needed to honor the good fortune of Lilly being okay to help heal my frayed nerves.

> **Mom Story**
>
> For 45 minutes at the ranch, I had not known whether or not she was going to live, and it was another 45-minute wait at the hospital before I found out that the dose was not toxic.

A friend reminded me of one of her children's accidents. Although she had "carved out a 'safety zone' for the kids" in her in-law's house, one of her toddlers ate some lead buckshot that had been used as weights for the electric train. Who would have thought that lead buckshot would be in the train? She said, "I second-guessed myself for years. It didn't do any good, but I worried constantly about the long-term effects. In the end, all we can do is thank God that we have the healthy, happy children we have, and do our best without overprotecting them or making them afraid to take chances. Anyway, you know what a great mom you are. You have such great kids. Be confident in that."

The Assistant Rector had a different take on it: "I can only imagine being in that place of unknown—when your body is all geared up to deal with a crisis, and yet your knowledge and resources will only let you deal so far. What a helpless feeling, and what a wonderful place to realize that God is with you." Their responses lifted my heart, and I felt better. It still took me another week or so to regain my confidence in my parenting and a few more to stop having nightmares.

Facing Miscarriage

So many hopes and dreams are tied up in the news of a pregnancy. In addition, many women who have a miscarriage still have the nausea and swelling of a normal pregnancy. They may feel the symptoms of pregnancy for a while even though their fetus is no longer viable or they have lost the baby. Many have also undergone painful, heart-wrenching infertility treatment.

Chris, a veteran of infertility treatments, joined an infertility support group to help her cope with the losses and dashed dreams. As a healing exercise, each member of her group wrote about her infertility experience. Here is an excerpt from Chris's arduous journey through loss and hope:

> The next several days were terrible for me. The waiting was agony and it was very close to Christmas. My Christmas spirit was gone and I didn't want to do anything but go and see how our little baby was doing. My husband came with me this time and the doctor found the baby had no heartbeat. Our dreams for the future were dashed. The best thing the doctor could offer us was sympathy and an appointment for a DNC to get the miscarriage over with.

After yet another miscarriage,

> . . . we got pregnant, much to the surprise and joy of all involved. We held our breaths while we waited to get past the hard first eight weeks, only to discover that the embryo had stopped developing and there was no detectable heartbeat. On the day of the DNC, as I sat crying in the chair, I asked the doctor to do a final ultrasound. At this point, the doctor found growth and a fetal pole, but still no heartbeat. No one could understand how the embryo could have grown if it was dead. So again, we decided to wait. I don't remember how long it was after that I started bleeding.

After four years of dealing with the tragedy of miscarriage, Chris finally got pregnant with her son a few months later. As we all know, not everyone is so lucky that they can even have one child. But what can you do to help with the loss?

Do an Amazon search and select some books that appeal to you, or go to the self-help section of the library. A book like *Pregnancy after a Loss: A Guide to Pregnancy after a Miscarriage, Stillbirth or Infant Death* by Carol Cirulli Lanham offers practical advice. *When Your Baby Dies Through Miscarriage or Stillbirth (Hope and Healing Series)* by Louis A. Gamino and Ann T. Cooney or *I'll Hold You in Heaven: Healing and Hope for the Parent Who Has Lost a Child*

Through Miscarriage, Stillbirth, Abortion, or Early Infant Death by Jack Hayford focus on your emotional state of mind and the healing process. Another highly recommended book is *Surviving Pregnancy Loss: A Complete Sourcebook for Women and Their Families* by Rochelle Friedman, MD and Bonnie Gradstein, MPH.

Once again, the Postpartum Support International website at www.postpartum.net offers resources, local and international support groups and a library. The books listed in their library are found at www.postpartum.net/bookstore.html. For a more personal treatment, *The Mother-to-Mother Postpartum Depression Support Book* by Sandra Poulin offers a collection of short pieces by moms who have experienced PPD.

What do you say to someone who loses a child? According to my guests on the "Honoring Grief" show, acknowledge the circumstances, but don't tell the bereaved parent that you know how she/he feels—because you don't. National organizations like Compassionate Friends or local organizations like the Bay Area's Kara, offer support for both adults and children. Liz Powell suggests that much of the healing is in sharing the experience with others who are "inside the experience." What is most helpful is just allowing the bereaved person to talk it out and to acknowledge that it is a difficult time. Platitudes such as: "you can always try for another child," or "it must have been meant to be," don't really help despite any good intentions.

The Death of a Loved One

There are few adversities in life tougher than this one. My sister-in-law Bernie, a mother of four, died just a few hours after my fourth child, Lilly, was born. A brain tumor. Boom. Bernie was gone. But Lilly had come. These are the cycles of life. Writing about Bernie's death helped me to put things in perspective. A journal can be a handy tool to find clarity or perspective.

I have several friends whose children have died, and I often think of these friends. One lost her child full term. It was a fluke. Several years later she told me, "There is not a day that goes by that I don't think of [Ellie]." Another had a child who was born with all of her organs reversed except for her heart. During her first year of life, she required numerous operations and two liver transplants. Her mother, Susan, often worried "what is Katie's life going to be like?" with all of these operations. Her baby was in the NICU more often than not. Still, her eyes and face lit up when she saw people, when she looked at the mobile floating above her, and when her parents and nurses sang and talked to her. She was present, no doubt about it.

Baby Katie passed away around the time of her first birthday. Though Susan was grieving, she realized that she still had a three-year-old daughter and a husband who needed her. Susan found support groups through the hospital and her own networks. She also got her daughter the help she needed as she grieved over her lost sister. These kinds of things helped her to move forward through the pain and not be alone in it.

I have held onto something I heard at Katie's funeral because it helps me to make sense of things. Her husband, Steve, said that Baby Katie had done so much for the world in one small year. "She touched so many lives and brought families together."

Nina, a working mother of two young children, lost her husband to leukemia a few years ago. His demise was rapid. They had actually just moved back to their native country when he began to frequently get sick. Thinking he might have malaria, he had his blood drawn and tested. "One day everything was fine and the next, it wasn't." They moved back to the United States to get the medical treatment they wanted and read everything they could get their hands on. The only cure was a bone-marrow transplant. With a positive outlook and ready to try their best to beat the odds, they set up bone-marrow drives in different cities, garnering support along the way.

After a failed partial-match transplant, they left their support network behind and moved with his parents to another city to be near a top cancer-research hospital. Those were long months. Each day, tests in the hospital. Each day, bad news. "For a long time I lived one day at a time. We'll just get through this day." They had to keep two apartments because her husband's immune system was wiped out by the treatment, and he had to be isolated as much as possible from germs. She would shuttle back and forth between both apartments to tend to him and to the children. The twins were three then and very isolated. "They couldn't go anywhere outside because if they got sick, they couldn't be around their father. We would take them to the parks when other kids weren't there" so "they needed me even more."

After her husband's death, Nina and her two children moved back to where they had friends and she had work. She took some time off from work for a while and gave herself time to grieve: "I was not functional." Working out helped her, so she joined Team in Training to train for her first marathon. "I really enjoy working out. It keeps me together." By being part of a training team, she has exercise buddies in place and a welcome distraction. "I get to listen to their lives and stories or I can walk alone at a different pace" and think about him.

> **Tips and Tools from Moms in the Trenches**
>
> Tools you can use when dealing with a terminal illness or life-changing diagnosis:
> - Research and recruit. Research the illness, cures, and experts. Recruit others to help you research. Print everything out or mail to those willing to help you tackle this overwhelming task. Create a website to coordinate your efforts and keep everyone updated on areas already researched so that others can go after new ones.
> - Spirituality or meditation. Find some time to be still, to think, to feel. Try to be open to new avenues of prayer and faith or rekindle old ones. In this time of despair, when many feel less connected to their spirituality, you can even pray for the willingness to be open. Walk or sit in a rock garden, in a park or on a grassy hill; listen to soothing music in the car; read some inspiring quotes, mediations, or faith-based texts. Allow others to pray for you or to put you and your loved ones on a prayer list.
> - Use your available resources. If social workers, nurses, counselors offer to talk or to listen, try to let them. What can you lose? They have experience and tools that could be helpful. This goes for your children, too.
> - Bring on the mantras. One day at a time. One moment at a time. One blood test at a time. Break the day down to something manageable.
> - Positive outlook. Reframe the situation whenever you can. Pull out your gratitude lists. Your smile or positive outlook, whenever possible, can boost the morale of those who may need it most.
> - Allow support networks, friends, and family to help. Write down things that still have to get done and let others help. Remember, they want to help you; give them concrete ways to do so.

- Talk it out. Share your fears and concerns with others. Give your children the space to talk it out . . . and to cry.
- Exercise when you can to naturally release some of the tension and anxiety.

Though most of her family is in another country, Nina has chosen to remain in the United States where she has established herself professionally and can provide for her kids and her extended family. She has also built a strong support network from work and graduate school friends as well as her grief support group. "I have many close friends here who can help me out and take the kids if I need it, anytime. I don't ask them very often, but I always know that I can."

Nina has some close friends who are father figures to her children. She has also signed her children up for the national organization Big Brother/Big Sister but is still on the wait list.

Ultimately, Nina strives to keep life in perspective. "I want the children to form strong social bonds. I don't mind if my kid is a hairdresser or a waitress. I want them to have a passion for life, to enjoy the day, to take this enjoyment home at the end of the day." Life is about living in the moment for that is all you have.

At some point, we all lose our parents. Sometimes the illness is long and drawn out, other times it is sudden as in a heart attack. Either way, we will run through the stages of grief in our own sequence: denial, anger, bargaining, letting go, and acceptance. We will also pass through each stage when we are ready. Maria brought up a behavior that has stayed with me. A year after her husband's mother died, he was on a real tear one day and unusually angry about some minor car

Mom Story

The grief support group "helps me say I am messed up but I am okay. It helps to see others struggling." She and the children also continue to meet with other families who have lost a parent. "One day my son came home upset. He said, 'But my dad will never get to come see me in school.' It is important for him to be around other children who have to deal with this also."

trouble. When he slammed the car door and pounded the car with his fists, she realized that this was not about the car but about something more. When he was ready to talk later in the day, he said he was angry with his mother for dying. He still missed her.

We have long histories with our parents, and so a parent's death can bring out unexpectedly strong and complex emotions. Guilty feelings about things left unsaid or undone can surprise and haunt you. The cause doesn't have to be especially momentous for the feelings to be powerful; in fact, often it's something simple from everyday life. One mother of two who recently lost her father said, "I feel guilty that he never got the homemade dumplings that he wanted." Another said that her dad had wanted a spicy Indian dish that she never got around to making because it takes awhile. "Right after he died, I found a box of the ingredients. I could have made it from the box and it would have been so easy."

Dierdra's older child experienced a lot of loss at an early age between the deaths of family members and pets, so Dierdra and her husband decided it was important to go outside of the home for some help. They wanted to find someone their child could talk with openly. The therapist helped their daughter address her worries, fears, and sense of loss. Books also helped Dierdra, her husband, and their daughter open up to each other. Having a passage to discuss, or an insight from someone else's story, gave them a way to start talking about their issues and emotions without feeling self-conscious.

> **Mom Story**
>
> "My grief comes in waves. Sometimes memories get triggered by something. It is as if there is an elephant on my chest and it's hard to breath at times." —Nina

Consider taking a look at some of these books, organizations, or websites to get your hands on some concrete material. Kara has put together an extensive categorized resource list for bereaved adults and children which can easily be found at www.sportofmotherhood.com/tools/htm. For additional resources and organizations recommended by Kara, go to www.kara-grief.org/help_advice.htm#section3. In addition, www.compassionbooks.com offers over 400 resources that help children and adults handle grief. There are many different categories from which to choose. Some excellent books to consider are: *On Death and Dying: What the Dying Have to Teach Doctors, Nurses, Clergy and Their Own Families*, by Elisabeth Kübler-Ross; *When Bad Things Happen to Good People* by Harold S. Kushner; *Tear Soup* by Pat Schwiebert, Chuck Deklyen and Taylor Bills; and *How to Go on Living When Someone You Love Dies* by Therese A. Rando. There are many more.

What about the death of a pet? For many people, pets are family members. They cherish them, and honor them when they die with a burial ceremony of some kind. When our mini-lop bunny, Jasmine, died, the kids and I each made a cross for her out of sticks, leather thong, beads, rocks, and markers to mark her gravesite. They were also consoled by the poem, "Rainbow Bridge," which our vet gave us. There are wonderful children's books that you can read with your child on this topic: *Cat Heaven and Dog Heaven*, by Cynthia Rylant, and *Lifetimes: A Beautiful Way to Explain Death to Children*, by Bryan Mellonie and Robert Ingpen, are good places to start.

Tips and Tools from Moms and Dads in the Trenches

After the death of a loved one
- Join a grief support group. Your hospital will point you to a local one. If none are available to you locally, join a support group on the Internet. Check out the ones for families, too. Your kids could benefit from meeting with or messaging other kids who have also lost a parent or sibling.
- Get some counseling both for yourself and for your children. It can only help.
- Keep your own journal. Log in your feelings and triggers. Document your memories and stories. Write about your struggles. You can learn a lot from your writing and also see progress where you may feel none otherwise. Keep a family journal. Have kids do entries, too. Talk about the high and low of each day.
- On holidays and birthdays, write a note and tape it to a balloon. Let it go and watch it disappear into the sky.
- Plant a vine, plant, or tree in his/her honor.
- Write notes or letters to your lost loved one.
- Work out. Exercise is a physical release. Tap into those endorphins. You may sleep better at night when your body is physically tired.

- Join a training group for some camaraderie, encouragement, accountability, and distraction. Distract yourself even more by picking a race to train for. Use support networks available like Team in Training (Leukemia) for marathons or Breast Cancer for walking events.
- Practice breathing exercises. One helpful website that offers exercises and classes is www.ArtofLiving.org. Change your frame of mind in the moment.
- Be gentle with yourself. Edit your schedule. Give yourself time to grieve. Some days putting a good meal on the table is enough.
- Give yourself breaks when you can. Add some childcare or babysitting time so that you have some time to regroup, to get the help you need, to heal, to move on. Then you can be fully present for your children.
- Acknowledge your mood each day. Some days are really terrible. Some days are okay. It helps to accept who you are and where you are.

Ongoing Challenges

Ongoing challenges are situations that introduce a constant, long-term change into our lives. The most common are raising special needs children, dealing with personal health issues, becoming a suddenly single mom (either through death or divorce) and battling cancer or diabetes. This wasn't what you signed up for, but you are now a part of a club you would never have voluntarily joined. So what do you do?

Raising Challenging Children

Are you raising challenging children or children with special needs, genetic issues, serious allergies, illnesses, or disabilities? How do you manage to rally each day, or do you? Where do you go when you feel overwhelmed? Kim, a mother of three, worked full time and part time while raising her family until she and her husband realized that they had two children with special needs. "I have one child who is high-functioning autistic, one who has ADD, and my third is a freebie. Some days are harder than others, but I talk to the man above and ask for patience and guidance. And I talk to my girlfriends." She finds her strength and patience for the day in prayer and support.

Jessica, a working mother of two, has one child with Down's Syndrome. "The commitments I have are based on work or our children. Many of our commitments are based on Will's needs. We have numerous commitments each week that are based on trying to support him to be the best he can be." She has a career that she loves which also offers "stimulation from adults on a consistent basis," financial incentives, as well as a "nice break for me." She prioritizes carefully and limits commitments to stay on top of things. Another mom of an eight-month-old with Down's keeps from mapping out the future. Instead, she tries to be in the moment. Who knows what challenges or victories the future will bring?

Robyn O'Brien, a mother of four, has a child with a life-threatening food allergy. When she launched into research mode, she realized how little awareness there was about food allergies and accident prevention. So she harnessed her energy and resources and founded AllergyKids, www.allergykids.com, which has product information, allergy education, and a research component.

Roberta Pagon, MD, Professor and Principal Investigator of GeneTests, recommends the following resources for genetic issues, tests, and support groups. To learn more about dealing with a range of genetic disorders or to find specific support groups, go to www.geneticalliance.org. If you are looking for a directory of genetic laboratories and how to use genetic testing, go to www.genetests.org. By searching on the Internet, you can get the most current medical research.

Suddenly Single Moms

Single moms can have the weight of the world on their shoulders. As Nina points out, it's *hard* for one person to manage everything that a family requires:

> I know that I cannot be a father and a mother to my children. . . . I feel guilty at times because I don't have enough energy for my kids all the time. Being a single parent is a lot of work. I am making all of the choices, even over mundane things like, 'What do we do this weekend?' or 'How do I plan

our summer?' I have all the financial issues, the investment choices. I need to buy a house now. It's a nightmare. So many things.

As a single mom, you do all that Nina describes, then add in dating and meeting potential partners while contending with a positive or negative reaction from the kids. All the balls are in the air, and you have to catch them.

If you have been married for a while, you and your partner probably divided up some of the responsibilities. Fear may be your biggest enemy right now because it can paralyze you. It's time to get a plan and get moving. Take a piece of paper and divide it into three columns. Assess all of your current responsibilities by writing them all down in the first column on the left.

Now look for the areas of weakness. Where do you feel less likely to have mastery over a task? Write those weak areas down in the second or middle column. To cope with them, you can either learn or delegate. Think about how you can learn the skills you need to be competent in those areas or whom you can turn to for help (paid or not) handling them.

Write the names of potential people, mentors, and types of classes that you might need in the third column. Finally, go back to your strategic plan and add this on. Break goals down into manageable bites and begin your research and your phone calls.

Remember to identify your support networks and use them. No need to go this alone. A little company and encouragement can go a long way.

Books like *The Complete Single Mother: Reassuring Answers to Your Most Challenging Concerns* by Andrea Engber and Leah Klungness or *The Single Mother's Survival Guide* by Patrice Karst give practical information for running a household and managing finances, custody agreements, and payments. *Single Mothers by Choice* by Jane Mattes or *How to Turn Boys into Men without a Man Around the House: A Single Mother's Guide* by Richard Bromfield and Cheryl Erwin offer topic-specific advice and encouragement. Check out all that the National Organization for Single Mothers at www.singlemothers.org has to offer. From "Recommended Reading" to "Divorced and Dating" to "Newsletters" and "Discussion Groups," I think you will find something that addresses your situation.

Tips and Tools from Moms in the Trenches: Suddenly Single

- Join singles groups. Presbyterian churches often have non-denominational programs for meeting other single people and have single moms support networks in place. Jewish Community Centers always have a wealth of resources and support, usually for the community at large to use. Ask around. Check your local paper for groups related to your interests.
- Meet people through shared interests: sports activities such as volleyball, hiking, biking, tennis, or running groups; the arts; book clubs.
- Get financial advice. Get some investment or financial advice online at www.myfinancialadvice.com, which has been recognized by *Newsweek*. You can talk to a live advisor by phone or email. Or take a class or two at your local community college.
- Fuel up. Identify some long-term interests and honor them. Sign up for a class in your area of interest like Renaissance art, beginners photography, French cooking, mystery writing, or Journalism 101.
- Get empowered. Get someone to teach you how to change your own tire or oil. Same goes for learning how to use a power drill so that you can hang whatever you want—shelves, pictures, coat hooks. Learn how to program the stereo, VCR, or TIVO if you don't already know how.
- Get grounded. Start going to Yoga.
- Make decisions. Try not get paralyzed because you feel overwhelmed. Make some decisions to move forward. If you make a poor decision, then learn from it. Don't beat yourself up. You will be more informed the next time around. Try not to make big decisions when you are amped up about something. You can always say, "Let me get back to you with an answer in 24 hours."
- Use those support groups. "Stitch and Bitch" (an all-women's sewing circle) is popular and therapeutic for a reason!
- Start or join a grown-up game night. Whether it's Bunko™, Cranium™, Rummikube™ or cards, have some group fun around a game of chance.
- Become involved. Put a little time into outreach, help someone else, build community, and gain some perspective.

Moms Who Get Sick

What does the family do when a mother gets sick? Friends, family, religious groups, schools, and community organizations will often pitch in to help with practical and emotional issues, but the mom also needs her own customized support. One mom of two who was recently diagnosed with breast cancer has been blessed with prayer groups at her house. These can become powerful healing exercises for all involved. Another held weekly twelve-step meetings at her house since she could not make it out to the meetings. Edit wherever possible. What can you take off your and your family's to-do or activity list?

If you are sick, you don't need to be on the phone all day explaining what is happening. You can streamline medical updates to friends and family and that way conserve your precious energy. First, pick a person who can be the contact. He or she can write out the latest medical information and send it to a designated email list. On this list, he or she can also help friends understand that you prefer email to phone calls because updating and reassuring friends and family on the phone is too draining.

For the friends who want to help out, the designated contact can also post a wish list of helpful and needed items. For example: need someone to take me to and from certain doctor's appointments, would like fresh assorted vegetables from Farmer's Market periodically (will be reimbursed), need size 5 Pampers diapers and Huggies wipes weekly from Costco (will be reimbursed), could use some help with school or activity pickups for kids on Wednesdays and Fridays. Friends can be helpful in practical ways and ease the mother's load.

Contending with your own health limitations can be overwhelming. Where do you go for support? Mothers groups or discussion or chat groups on the Internet can be helpful resources and places to connect. Search for your topic or concern, connect and reach out.

Cancer? Do a Google search on cancer and pick the links of your choice such as www.cancer.org, which offers "Facts, Resources and Support" from the American Cancer Society. The Y-ME National Breast Cancer Organization at www.y-me.org is another one to use, especially if you have just been diagnosed with breast cancer. The NBCC or National Breast Cancer Coalition at www.nbcc.org.au has information on advocacy groups, quality care, drug trials, non-profit information, and more. Get informed.

Some mothers like the anonymity of the Internet. Others enjoy the speed and directness and ability to have a conversation at any time of the day or night. Anna regularly uses Salon.com's "Mothers Who Think" to find a meeting of minds. Go to www.salon.com and search for "Mothers Who Think" to get archived articles and current discussion groups. Another mother uses one of the online breast cancer support groups for herself. She can talk with other women who have or have had breast cancer from her very own bed. "With the Internet, I don't even have to leave my bed to talk about my concerns and get some reassurance and ideas when possible." In addition, she is able to get some of the latest research and be proactive or at least well informed about the options regarding her healthcare.

What about something like diabetes? Go to www.diabetes.com or www.diabetes.org to get tools and strategies to manage your disease or go to www.thebeehive.org/health for good, useful information about diabetes and the kinds of experiences we have discussed in this chapter, those that leave you feeling like you've been hit by a truck, can teach you lessons you would never have learned otherwise. You can never brush off such an experience, but you can rise up through it. In the middle of the change and upheaval that marks every loss, it can help enormously to have some general strategies to help you lighten the load. Here, again, is my list:

1. Write. Write in a journal or write a letter or email that you may or may not send out. Try some poetry or jot down some lyrics. Writing something down can also help you to feel like you are "honoring the death."

2. Read self-help books such as *On Grief and Grieving: Finding the Meaning of Grief Through the Five Stages of Loss* by Elisabeth Kübler-Ross and David Kessler or a novel such as Lolly Winston's *Good Grief* to better understand what you are experiencing. Check out Kara's categorized resource list for bereaved adults and children which can easily be found at www.sportofmotherhood.com/tools/htm. Search Amazon at www.amazon.com and check out reader critiques and ratings. Ask your pediatrician or librarian for books related to your topic that are age-appropriate for your children.

3. Ask for help. Ask your doctors, pediatrician or librarian for suggested reading. Let your friends help you out in manageable ways.

4. Find or start a support group. Ask your doctor for local topic-specific support groups. Do a Google search on the Internet. If you can't find a support network that meets your needs, start one on the Internet or locally. Post a notice and see who comes. You can meet in neutral, populated zones such as coffee shops or bookstores. Talk about it with others in your support network.

5. Practice H.A.L.T. Try not to get too Hungry, Angry, Lonely, or Tired.

6. Look for the positive. What do you currently have that you are grateful for? Make a gratitude list every night. You can do it in your head or write it down.

7. Be kind to yourself. Give yourself flowers, a treat, or a bubble bath to help soothe the pain.

8. Relax your goals. Extend deadlines if necessary or take items off your to-do list.

9. Allow time for grief and healing. Give yourself time to cry and to heal. If you bottle your feelings up, you will have to deal with them later, or they may come out in unhealthy ways.

10. Lessons learned: Review your experience. Is there anything you would do differently if you pass this way again? Remember, hindsight is 20/20. Don't beat yourself up, but maybe you can do a few things differently the next time you face adversity.

11. Teach. You can help others both informally or formally when they go through a similar situation. You can help as needed or lead a support group or give a talk. Educate others so that they can learn what to watch for and where to get the help they need.

Wrap-Up

Each tragedy is unique, but one thing that helps you deal with any tragedy is support. Whether your truck arrives in the form of accident, miscarriage, death, divorce, or illness, others can help you get through your pain and loss. In some situations, simply the listening ear of a friend or spouse is sufficient, but with more challenging situations, you may need the company of others who are in similar situations or the ear of a trained therapist.

Support networks work two ways: As you are supported, you also help another person by allowing them to comfort or help you. You can also learn some practical coping strategies from others who face similar struggles and challenges. Sometimes it is enough just to know that you are not unique and that there are others who are sad, lonely, and angry or feel helpless. At other times, you can teach others how you worked through a trying time. As you build a community and share experience, strength, and hope, you can lighten your load and your heart.

CHAPTER 9

Crossing the Finish Line and Getting the Goody Bag

> ▶ R U able 2 celebrate small victories?
> ▶ R U looking 4 some traveling strategies?

Crossing a finish line usually feels pretty good. There's satisfaction in it, no matter how long the race or how significant the task. We feel a sense of accomplishment because we have completed something. We are relieved that, despite our fears and challenges, we did it! After a race is run or a goal completed, both a runner and a mother enjoy some kind of goody bag. A runner's goody bag usually contains the latest samples of running fuel, magazine clippings, training advice, news of future races, and other running products. A mother's goody bag can hold many wonderful things. She may find of a boost of energy and inspiration mixed with her feeling of accomplishment. There might be respect and appreciation from others for what she is doing. Sometimes she finds a sense of gratitude for the many ways she has been blessed. Her goody bag may yield up a prize of more time for herself or delight in family and friends or a feeling of earned downtime.

At the finish line, we should first cherish our success before we get hung up on how we might have traveled the course differently. Savor and enjoy your success; you've earned it! You've learned something, you've got new information, but it will keep. Save it for tomorrow. As a runner can train differently for the next race, a mother can factor the new information into her mom marathon training to better suit her and her family dynamic. But first, enjoy the finish.

Small Victories

Motherhood is cyclical. The clothes always need to be washed, the family fed, the dishes and house cleaned, and the toys or gear picked up. Concrete linear goals can give you small victories and show you that you are making some headway in the mother-load.

Your weekly finishes can be about projects completed (journal pages entered, books read, rooms decluttered or reorganized) or they can be about meeting a time goal for that week. As you record personal time or amount of hours spent on a project, remember that staying true to your progress is one of your best goals. Keep doing and you are doing something good.

movement = progress = success

This equation is true even if your movement is creating the time and space for downtime, meditation, naptime, book reading, sewing, or yoga! The small victories can boost your enthusiasm so that you tackle the following week with a renewed sense of purpose and vigor.

Enjoying the Mom Marathon and Crossing the Finish Line

One of your goals is to enjoy the sport of motherhood. By enjoying the journey and the process, you are living in the present. Your children will never be the same age again; savor the moment. By setting goals for your future, you gain a better idea of where you are headed without losing your full connection to the present.

Just as you have set the course, you can assess and adapt it as needed. What daily, weekly, and monthly finish lines you set will depend on your objectives and personal timetables. Reassessing is essential! Maybe you met a deadline at work or on a volunteer project, but had to admit afterwards that the pace was too fast and triggered more stress than expected. You can approach the next project differently, taking into account your new information about what type of pace works with your family dynamic.

> **MOM TIP**
>
> I like to keep in mind the idea of pacing myself for life. If I go too fast and do too much, I will burn out. If I pace myself well, I have more stamina and can do my project well without its taking a toll on the family. That means not too fast and not too slow.

We have already talked about the dangers of over commitment and how to streamline your day and your family schedule. Those ideas are applicable here. Remember, each balancing quest is personal and each journey unique.

Nurturing Joie de Vivre

Celebrating small victories is also about finding pleasure in your life and allowing it to prosper. How can you nurture your *joie de vivre* or joy of living? Sometimes you just have to release a pressure valve. How about through humor? Go back to your humor resources in Chapter 6. Let yourself enjoy those simple things that bring you pleasure, like sipping a fine tea, or counting toes or admiring the sunset.

The Gift to Be Simple

Simple, fun things to do with kids and bring out the kid in you:
- Create a laughing library. Help the kids "collect" the funny family stories and retell them.
- Jump in puddles with your kids and see who makes the biggest splash.
- Gather some bread and feed some ducks at a local pond. Feeding birds can be incredibly satisfying for all ages.
- Bring out the bubbles with your kids. Wet your hand and try to put your hand into a large bubble without popping it. Bubbles bring out the kid in all ages.
- Go to a local craft store such as Michael's and see what draws your interest. Perhaps some cloth bags/t-shirts and fabric paints, or some beading, soap, or candle projects get your attention.

- Sponge paint or stencil a wall in your house with your kids.
- Go to the beach and chase the waves, build a sand castle, or find and try to identify one of each kind of shell or rock on the beach (using a pocket guide).
- Take a hike and try to identify flowers, fauna, bugs, or rocks along the way (using pocket guides).
- Fly a kite or go watch the kite flyers. Stunt kite antics entertain all.
- Take a trip to an amusement park or boardwalk. If you go with another adult, be sure to take a turn on a roller coaster to get your adrenaline going!
- Pull out a board game that appeals to you as well as the kids. Create appropriate restrictions for yourself so that you may play competitively with them and challenge yourself as well.
- Write a funny story together in a round-robin format. Each person gets to make up one sentence and then passes the story on to the next person, who develops a sentence based on the previous one.
- Do some Mad Libs™ as a family. Even if some of the kids aren't old enough to identify parts of speech, they can still make up words and the results will be funny.
- Keep the kids up late one night to look at the stars and identify constellations while sipping hot chocolate.
- Do a 1000-piece puzzle together. Smaller kids can do their own puzzle next to you, but even ages five and up can help a bit with yours. If you do the puzzle on a felt mat, you can roll it up and put it away until the next time you are able to work on it.
- Go rollerblading. Throw in hockey sticks, some moms and kids, and have some real fun.
- Climb a tree with your child and sit up high for awhile.

Find the kid in you. Where do you feel light and carefree? For many for us, a change of location helps us to leave the work—whether it is housework, paid work, or volunteering—behind. An activity such as flying kites, collecting shells, or going to an amusement park with the kids could do the trick. Annie, who enjoys going to Disneyland as much as her children, says, "Basically I am just a big kid, but I can drive and have a credit card!" **Make time to play**, and you'll have the interest and energy to pursue your passions.

The Goody Bag

Just as a runner gets a goody bag from the race organizers, I have some "goodies" for you that can help you with your mom marathon. I like to fill a mother's goody bag with boosts of inspiration and encouragement. Moms in training need that. Here I have some handy tips on traveling with kids and managing multiple children.

MOM TIP

Sometimes you can feel so overwhelmed by trip prep that you don't even want to go. You can actually train yourself to get in a particular frame of mind that limits the dread and anxiety and enables you to enjoy the trip.

I. Traveling with Kids

Are you taking a family trip or going on vacation?

This is a useful distinction for trip planning. Many moms I interviewed describe "family trips" as travel to spend time with their extended family and "vacations" as travel to be with their nuclear family. If you are planning a trip, ask yourself if it's a family trip, a vacation, or both.

What does vacation mean to you? How about to your spouse? How about to your family? These can be very different things.

Shana McLean Moore, a writer and guest on my TV show, has a great take on vacation planning for her family:

> The way I see it, you need to ride the wave that the gods of the currents send you. In my current phase of life, with kids ages eight and ten, this still means that I'm best off with vacations designed specifically for children. Of course, different people define vacation differently. Many adults shudder at the thought of an overpriced Disney extravaganza, but it's my dream come true. After all, I could truly have a good time in someone's garage if the people I was with were happy and I didn't have to cook.

To me, vacation means furrow-free days of family fun and relaxation. At this stage of life, I have no desire to do a family hike up the Himalayas. I just wouldn't want to drag the kids along to fulfill my personal agenda. It would not be fun, relaxing, or at all furrow-free for me to cajole my kids up a mountain. I'd wind up carrying both their packs and my own just to hear the whining stop. There will be plenty of time for those kinds of trips when the kids are grown and going their own way. Until then, color me Disney or at a house at the beach where I can read a book while they collect shells until they're pinker than a crab's leg. That's a wave that I can ride smoothly to the shores of family harmony.

Travel to be with grandparents, cousins, aunts and uncles, nieces and nephews is a big part of building family life and keeping families together. You could be traveling for a big occasion—like a wedding, graduation, or major birthday—or just to get together and touch base. It's a great tradition, too, because families can be so spread out these days. These family trips can be awesome ways to build relationships and memories.

Many moms also talked about the cost involved in trying to please everyone else, whether that is relatives who are expecting a visit or kids clamoring for an amusement park. Cara, a working mom of two, has learned to "balance the number of extended family trips and vacations with just family. There is a difference. Make time for your own family." Otherwise, later in the year, she and her husband are resentful. They have not taken care of their own FQT (Family Quality Time) needs.

Have Baby, Will Travel. Have Baby, Wait to Travel

The expression "Have baby, will travel" is apt. Some folks love to be on the go with kids in tow. If you aren't willing to leave your house to travel with kids, you won't see much of your extended family or the world at large; however, many families decide to travel when the kids get older, are easier to travel with, and can appreciate the trip more. It is your call. The right way is what works for you. If you do decide that you are up for some trips, read through the strategies below to see if any are applicable to your family dynamic. They can help you plan an age-appropriate trip.

- **Assess your energy level and your children's ages and stages.** Infants up to the stage of crawling are quite portable; however, taking a one-year-old on a plane is a different story. It is difficult but doable if you are up for it, or if you and your partner can share the work. As soon as kids are old enough to sit and color, traveling with kids gets a whole lot easier.

- **Think about duration.** If you are thinking of flying coast to coast for a weekend trip with small children, you might decide "NOT"! If you go for a week or two, then you can give the kids time to adjust to the time change and new surroundings. They'll settle in.

- **Assess your plans for age-appeal.** Once you are there, what will the kids do? If your goal is to get in a lot of sightseeing and fine dining, then you probably want to find some childcare or take the kids when they are older.

- **Plan for the travel days.** Traveling is challenging, especially for young children. Keep the fun in the vacation by compartmentalizing travel (days one and seven, for example) and vacation (days two to six). Have different plans for optimizing everyone's experience on your travel days. Tip: You can pay each child $1 per travel day (i.e., in the car or on a plane) to reward them for teamwork. Their extra hands are often needed and good moods are helpful!

- **Have a game plan for traveling with a group or attending a large family gathering.** For example, have some plans for helping kids through buffet lines, knowing who is responsible for the kids, carrying paraphernalia back to the room at the end of each day, and getting a bit of quality time with your nuclear family. Know your or your partner's flexibility threshold to help daily group decision making go more smoothly.

- **Get into adventure mode.** Mishaps will happen. Take them on as challenges rather than problems. Keep the fun by finding the fun factor.

Know Your Flexibility Threshold

Some people are more adaptable to change, some less. Because travel disrupts our usual routines, it can really test our ability to cope with the minor changes that are part of most trips: different food, a lumpy bed, late nights, strange water, new people. We all know kids and adults who really love their routines. Understanding your own flexibility threshold is important when traveling with kids, and it's especially important to identify when traveling with kids with a group because group travel intensifies the pressures to adapt to others.

Ask yourself these questions to determine your flexibility. When traveling with a group, do you:

- want to help plan the schedule?
- go with the flow if someone else has mapped out the schedule?
- have a serious need for personal space and find ways for you and your family to escape?
- plan for some quality time with just your partner or your nuclear family?
- seek unstructured time?
- talk with your partner ahead of time about getting the kids through the buffet line or go over exit strategies in case your kids fall apart at the fourth long family dinner?
- plan for a way for you to get some exercise or alone time somewhere in the trip?

Look at your answers. What do you tend to do? Are you good at taking care of yourself, too, so that you do not become resentful and no fun to be around?

Traveling with a Group? Preserve some Family Time

When traveling with a group or with extended family, how do you set aside some time with your own family? If you are vacationing with extended family, you might feel bad about slipping away or not joining in every group activity. Let yourself off the hook. Explain what you're up to so no one is hurt or surprised, and then take the time you need. Combat the guilt-factor. Here are some ways to get those moments with your family:

- Give the group or grandparent-in-charge the heads up on your plans ahead of time.
- Ask your tour guide, camp counselor, or group leader for suggestions.
- Schedule a lunch or dinner just for your nuclear family.
- Slip away for an afternoon walk, swim, boat ride, or shopping excursion.

- Meet back in the hotel room or condo or tent for a board game or some basic R and R.

Make sure your partner and kids understand about "family time" so you don't undercut each other. Cara recommends: "Stay in your own hotel or condo room and have breakfast together. Go for a morning walk or swim." Make an effort to protect the time, and you make an effort to keep or stay connected.

Travel Tips and Tools from Moms in the Trenches

This list includes the greatest hits from my many interviews with moms on the topic of traveling with kids. Read and enjoy. Try them on for size: There's no formula here except what works for you.

1. **Travel Lists** — Many moms I interviewed used a checklist to keep packing and travel preparation under control. You can use a master list and adapt it to different trips, or keep specialized lists. Cara uses her computer to update her lists:

   > I have a pretyped list on my computer that I print off and use as a checklist for packing. Great for weekend getaways or when kids take trips with the grandparents. It saves me from making a new list every time. I have an airplane travel list as well, for trips that are a distance away.

   Sarah categorizes her packing lists by trip type (camping lists, ski lists, beach lists, East Coast lists) and keeps them on an Excel spreadsheet.

   > We have several [lists] depending on the destination. We usually start with a list and then cross off things we won't need for this trip. Greg usually packs the Food and Camping columns and I usually take the Clothes, Toys, and Accessories columns. I always think we take too much, so if we leave a couple of things behind we just have the adventure of living without them. Before we leave I ask myself, "do we have the really Important lifesaving stuff (like proper clothes for the weather, tickets for the flight)," and then I stop worrying about anything else.

Producing these kinds of lists may seem like a lot of work, and it is an up-front effort, but you just have to do it once and then adapt as you go. Having your lists on the computer makes that easy and quick. Referring to a tried-and-true checklist when you're leaving for a trip takes a lot of the anxiety out of the packing. Plus, when you keep it all in your head, it's harder to delegate!

2. **Good Attitude** — Set the tone of the trip. Try to limit travel anxiety to one day out and one day back (compartmentalize!). When you feel yourself start to worry, then try to think about something else. That can be hard, so practice it. Prepare for your travel days as you would train for a race. Try to get a good night's sleep two days prior to traveling. Everyone will benefit if you feel rested. You will be better equipped to handle the immediate challenges of sibling squabbles and diaper dashes.

    The same is true for your return trip: Don't let worry about travel details spoil your last couple of vacation days. If the clothes are dirty, people are having fun! Have a simple play for getting everything packed up. If you are flying, know your route to the airport and have a plan to leave on time.

3. **Realistic Itinerary** — Be realistic about your children's ages and stamina. Don't overschedule them or you on the trip. With younger kids, a good rule of thumb is one outing or activity a day. Anything more is a bonus given the mood and sleep needs of the day.

4. **Basics Preordering and Pre-Packing** — A little extra pre-trip organization can make your travels go more smoothly. Two weeks prior to a trip, place an order on a grocery delivery service such as Netgrocer at www.netgrocer.com. Order nonperishable items such as diapers, formula, Nutragrain bars, PB&J, crackers, and coffee to be shipped to your destination. These items can buy you some time before your first grocery store visit.

    A week prior to the trip, tackle the plane bags. Note: HIDE them or make them off-limits after they are packed. Otherwise, you will be redoing the work! If possible, use a small rolling suitcase as an extra plane bag filled with change of clothes for each young child, extra food, children's medicine and a thermometer, and extra diapers and wipes and/or formula, if you are still in that stage. These days you never know if you will miss a flight or connection.

Lugging a car seat around can take the shine off a good start. Having to tote two or three of them on top of suitcases and backpacks can perplex even the best travel engineer. They are absolutely necessary, but big and bulky. Our travel pro mom, Cara, recommends that you "take advantage of car seat services. Limos will hold or store your seats, and if you rent a car on the other end (most minivans have them built in), you can save yourself hauling car seats through airports. Also, car rental companies will rent car seats as well." Book ahead and go.

5. **Suitcase Strategies** — Pack lightly!! Here is Cara's advice:

> If you are going somewhere that has laundry facility, only pack a half a week's worth of clothing for everyone. Do a few loads midweek. Get each child his or her own suitcase with wheels, teach him how to pull it and make it his responsibility (my two- and five-year-olds can do it).

One mom of multiples recommends using plastic grocery bags to pack daily wardrobes. She packs each day's clothes for each child in one bag and labels the bag with the child's name. "They pull out the bag for the day and they are done." This strategy eliminates pulling clothes out of the suitcase and getting clothes mixed up. She also splits each person's clothes between two suitcases. "That way if a suitcase is lost en route, there are still clothes to wear."

6. **Personal Travel Backpacks for Each Child** — Give each child his own plane bag and nonperishable snack. Rolling backpacks are worth the investment if you don't have them. Even a three-year-old can pull one with encouragement and positive reinforcement. Older kids can pack their own bags. Vary entertainment items for the younger ones: a miniature Magna Doodle, pipe cleaners and large beads, a can of play dough, coloring book and crayons or markers, books with flaps, toy cars, a set of farm animals. Pack a surprise for each child during the travel day, whether it is a velvet art poster, an invisible ink book with questions or drawings, or a brainteaser toy. When possible, bring along some age-appropriate reading material that relates to your destination.

7. **Get into Adventure Mode** — Get in the mood for travel by thinking of the trip as an ADVENTURE. You are prepared. Now it is time to go with the flow and let go of some expectations. Some things WILL go wrong. Laugh about them and adapt and improvise. Take deep breaths and start your day over as needed.

8. **Clarify Expectations** — Make sure that everyone knows what kind of trip you are taking and what their responsibilities are on the trip. Clarifying trip expectations ahead of time really helps prevent misunderstandings. Divide up duties like help with meal times, kid control, cleanup, and bedtime. Allot enough personal time for each partner. Some vacation activities, like golf, are very time consuming: make sure to discuss those schedules ahead of time. Talk about expectations with in-laws ahead of time, too. Come up with a discreet signal that you and your partner can use to indicate it is time to call it quits for the night.

9. **Motivate Travel Cooperation** — I started paying each child $1 per travel day to reward them for rallying, helping without complaining and just being good travel sports. Sometimes it takes us two days to get to our destination, so they get $2, which is a big deal in my family. Even if a child melts down, I do not take the dollar away; rather I reinforce any positive, helpful, team spirit behavior. A travel day is not always that easy on kids, so why not give them a reward and some money to spend on the trip if they like?

10. **Keep Kids Entertained and Keep you Sane** — When visiting old friends, grandparents or relatives, you can pack a bag filled with Klutz craft kits, art supplies, some travel board games, a puzzle, two decks of cards, a pack of super balls, lace doilies (to color at table), an Escher coloring book (appealing to older kids), balloons, and a pump. Pull items out as needed for meal times and grown-up visits. Believe it or not, you might be able to actually sit and catch up with a friend or relative.

11. **Travel Fun: Journals, Games, Language Ideas** — For longer trips, kids can bring a large trip journal in which they can write, color and glue things. At times, I have copied maps of the new country and various destinations for my kids to glue in and plot

our course as we travel. On the trip, they collect museum stubs, brochures and local maps that they can glue into their journals. They also add postcards picked up from various sights so that they do not have to wait for pictures to be developed.

For more Travel Fun Ideas (travel journals, recyclable towns, and creating a new lingo such as "Disney Lingo"), go to Appendices C and D.

12. **Kids on the Move** — Here are some tips from one of my experienced traveling moms: "Bring an umbrella-style stroller, even if the child doesn't need it—it's great for hauling extra carry-ons and bags when a child gets tired."

    Plan periods of activity for the kids and there's a better chance they'll be able to sit still when they have to. Joe has a great plan for addressing kids' exuberant energy levels. He likes to "run them like crazy up and down the hallways. Tire them out before you get them on the plane." Use the airport play structures and kid zones. Build in extra time for mishaps.

13. **Keeping Track of Kids** — Matching neon or tie-dye t-shirts are mighty helpful. In one family I interviewed, the boys all wear neon t-shirts. The kids don't ask. The parents don't tell them why. It's to keep track of them of course! They also use neon light-up arm bands for night ball games. You can buy bands in bulk at stores like Oriental Traders and Party America.

    Leashes can work for younger ones. Hey, if your child does not mind, try using a leash. Some little kids are remarkably independent and prone to wandering. This is about your kid's safety!

14. **Sick Kids** — Be prepared to handle a sick kid; then, if everybody stays healthy, you're in clover. If you can carry a small but well-stocked first aid and cold remedy kit, you won't have to rush out to the pharmacy. Cara likes to "bring all medicines. My kids are often sick on trips. If you have the over-the-counter stuff handy it really helps."

15. **Returning Home** — Plan your travel dates so that you have at least one day to get your life back in order before you go back to work, the kids go back to school and you resume your other

engagements. Divide and conquer—have your spouse pick a few things to do to help get things squared away from the trip.

A number of interviewees recommended starting your return trip bright and early so that you arrive home with time to unwind and relax before you jump back into your home routine. It gives you time to get settled, go though mail, and get reoriented at home. It can make your reentry easier.

Here's a variation on the early return idea. It's just a little sneaky, but works like a charm. Let people think that you are coming home later than you really are. Or just don't announce your return . . . yet. That can give you a day or two of secret vacation at home. You can come back early and take the extra time to get resettled. Nettie likes to "not tell anyone we are there that next day so we can ease back into life—maybe even play a board game and keep the trip glow."

16. **Late Return** — If you come in late, tackle at least fifteen minutes of focused unpacking to get a jump on things and feel more oriented. Nettie has a great way to start the unpacking process:

> Even if I just get one large load of laundry in and get the suitcases to the right rooms, that works. I also bring one large plastic bag and put all dirty clothes in it and in one suitcase. That suitcase comes home and goes right into the garage where the washing machine is.

If you treat unpacking as a terrible chore, so will everyone else. Reverse that trend right away. Take it a little bit at a time and make it fun! Nettie likes to "reward everyone with a fun board game, card game or story time after unpacking a bit." Have dinner delivered. I call this finding the fun factor.

17. **Preventing Letdown** — Know your limits. How tired are you from the trip? You may be all talked out after visiting with family. After organizing a successful family trip, you may have zero energy left for other organizing activities. Take the time to recover. Give yourself space if you do not want to see people and be "on"—you need time to regroup and recharge. On the other

hand, if you've been relaxing on a beach somewhere, you may be ready to jump right back into the thick of things.

18. **A Genevieve Blog on Reentry** — I had just returned from a road trip with the kids and was bone-tired for a few days. Though I knew that I would be tired upon my return, I did not expect to be that tired. It was more about "reentry" into my life again.

    When I get away from the daily pace of life, I can have a hard time reentering. It does not mean that my life is too busy; it just takes a few days to get back into the swing of things. I always have to remind myself of that at the end of a trip—or else my mom or a friend reminds me.

    Stepping away also helps me to assess and reprioritize. As I talked to both working moms and stay-at-home moms about reentry after vacation, I heard the same themes: reentering life, adjusting, getting used to the schedules again, and feeling out of sorts. Some of the full-time working moms felt particularly harried because they came home to a full work week, then packed something in on the weekend so that everyone felt like they had "had a vacation."

    I found my stride again, but it took me a few days longer to get fully back. During that time, I helped myself recharge by renting a movie for the kids and for me, reading a mystery, taking a nap or two, and editing our schedules wherever possible. I also revived by laughing about reentry with fellow moms—they just helped to put it all in perspective.

How about you? What do you do to recharge?

II. Managing Multiple Children

If you are raising multiple children, you can always draw on the model of a TEAM:

> **TEAM = Teamwork, Encouragement, Accountability, and Management**

Teamwork

Just as team players on a sports team help each other out and play together, families with multiples benefit from teamwork. The older kids can help the younger ones in a variety of ways. A four-year-old can help a one-and-a-half-year-old get dressed and get to the breakfast table. A four-year-old can also put milk or water in a sippy cup for a toddler and give it to her. A five-year-old can put waffles or toast in the toaster and use wooden tongs to pull them out when ready. An eight-year-old can put a three-year-old to bed with stories and a song while you focus on homework with a sibling. Be creative and assess your family's needs and abilities. Praise the kids for their help and even tell some friends about it to reinforce the helpful behavior.

You can also use charts and allowance to reward the children for their work. Some families decide upon a base allowance. Others say the allowance begins after the basic chores are done. They don't want the kids to feel like they have to be paid to do regular chores. Their help is just expected. Think about what would work best in your family and try it. You can also have bonus work. If sorting socks is a nightmare for you and you have a bucket of unmatched socks in your laundry room, the incentive of a penny a pair can make it fun for the kids and boost your morale.

Babysitting can also be extra. You can pay younger kids ages six and up 25 cents each for a half-hour of helping to watch and play with a younger sibling while you are in the house doing something else such as cooking a meal. Make the expectations clear. They have to stay with the younger sibling. If they don't want to do it or are "all done" in the middle of the time period, then they need to tell you, and that has to be okay with you since the goal is attentive supervision. If the younger child is a toddler, babysitting for fifteen-minute intervals is probably more appropriate. The babysitting at this age is more of a focused playtime that also enhances sibling relationships. So often in a family of multiples, the youngest goes along with the older kid schedules and activities. Babysitting time can encourage the older children to think more about what the youngest child likes to do. Children also take pride in being old enough to "babysit."

Encouragement

Just as you rally a team in a sport, you can rally your children to help out with the daily chores. Take the time to train them using **encouragement**, or positive reinforcement, and **accountability**, or consistent expectations. Visiting kids will help, too. That is the expectation.

Accountability

Kids can learn to do the work well. Chores such as feeding the pets, setting the table, unloading the dishwasher, putting out the recycling, making beds, sweeping the floors, sorting socks, putting away laundry, and unloading the car are manageable for kids and helpful to you! Kids become proud of their help or "chores." They learn to be accountable by consistently fulfilling their duties. When they help out the family, everyone can have more time to do fun things together.

Management

When managing multiples, a bit of extra organization or **management** goes a long way. In addition to a large color-coded family calendar, a posted daily calendar helps to keep everyone on track for the morning, homework and nighttime routines. Another tip: when the kids are beyond diapers, they can sleep in their clothes for the next day or can lay them on the floor to put on in the morning. Both approaches work; however, if you deal with a dawdler every morning and actually getting clothes on a body part takes numerous reminders, you may want to try the former approach for a while. If the child gets speedier, you can reward her by letting her get dressed in the morning. It is all in the marketing!

Streamlining activities benefits all. Combine errands whenever possible. Initiate or join carpools to help with activities. Limit activities per child. Both the children and the family need down time. Explain to the kids that they are lucky to have each other as playmates. Of course, you will have sibling squabbles, so pair up an older and younger rather than two older and two younger ones at times.

In a family with three or more children, finding one-on-one time for each child can be hard. Be sure to affirm what you are able to do. For example, you can stagger bedtimes by age so that you and your partner may at least have time to talk with an older child. Remind the child that this is his special time with Mom or Dad. By combining play dates, you can schedule some one-on-one time with another child. It can be easier to have a couple of friends over at the same time so that a sibling does not have to share a friend. Whichever child does not have a play date can have a special time with Mom or Dad. Reading a story, playing a board game, doing a craft or a cooking project can make it a focused and meaningful time for the two of you.

Expand the village. In the old days, it took a village to raise a child. I believe it is up to the modern mom to create her own village, especially if you are living away from family. Look for opportunities to expand your support network with child-friendly singles or empty-nesters. Before allowing private play dates, invite the older person along to the playground or over for playtime at your house. Make sure the person has the right temperament to deal with your children. If this works out, it gives your children extra individual attention and broadens the child's support network as well. Consider young married couples, too. Sometimes younger couples who are planning to have kids would love to get some practice. Be creative and stay aware of this possibility. If it works, it can be a win-win for both parties.

Wrap-Up

I hope that *The Sport of Motherhood's* Training Program has helped prepare you to make the most out of your weekly course and family dynamic. You've done some wonderful work along the way. Congratulations! Let's look at all you've accomplished. You looked at your personal mom marathon course and focused on some long-term goals. Then you clarified those long-term goals and objectives and figured out how to begin to bring them into the present. By setting up a strategic plan, you made time for new priorities and edited your schedule while keeping the family calendar in mind. You thought about what kind of support you need. Next, you began to target possible support networks and ways to develop and create a personalized support network to help you reach your goals. You learned to encourage teamwork at home, involving your family more fully in your mom marathon.

Once you decided on your course, you learned ways to train for your marathon, to fuel up, nurture yourself and create realistic manageable goals that set you up for success. You know how to readjust your goals if needed. You now have a whole bag of tools and tips to help you find endurance, pace for life, and prevent burnout. When you hit those inevitable walls, you know what to do and have ways to get around them. You even have some tools and resources for how to deal with some of life's tragedies.

Now you have crossed the first of many finish lines and can celebrate your success. You did it! You made it through this training course and have begun an exciting new stage in your life that will be filled with goody bags and celebrations. Remember, making the most out of your mom marathon is not so much about the ultimate race as it is the enjoying the course of the day. Run your mom marathon with some thoughtful planning, and you can do whatever your heart desires.

EXERCISES

Warm Up: Reflective Stretches

A. Do pre-trip logistics ever sap your enthusiasm for travel? _____

B. What does vacation mean?
   1. to you _____
   2. to your spouse _____
   3. to your family _____

Practice: New Skills

Assess Travel Readiness by Coming on Safari

Before planning a trip do you (circle the answers that apply to you):

1. assess your energy level and the children's ages and stages? **Yes or No**
2. think about duration? **Yes or No**
3. ask yourself if it is an adult or kid-oriented trip? **Yes or No**
4. compartmentalize travel days vs. vacation days? **Yes or No**

5. develop a game plan if traveling with a large group or extended family? **Yes or No**

6. pace yourself and your family while on the trip? **Yes or No**

Look at your answers. How many **Yes** answers did you circle? Compare your total with the score below and see which safari animal you are:

- 0–2 Ostrich: Your head is in the sand at times. You may often feel overwhelmed before, during, and after a trip—and not know why.

- 3–4 Monkey: You have some balance and give a trip some thought, some prep, some spontaneity, and some planning. You have a bit of mischief about you.

- 5–6 Leopard: You are a stellar strategizer and plan your trip with intention and purpose, matching objectives and needs, ages and stages.

Discover Your Flexibility Threshold

1. When traveling with a group, do you (circle the answers that apply to you):

    - want to help plan the schedule? **Yes or No**
    - go with the flow if someone else has mapped out the schedule? **Yes or No**
    - worry that you won't have your partner's full help on the trip? **Yes or No**
    - have a serious need for personal space and find ways for you and your family to escape? **Yes or No**
    - plan for some QT with just your partner or your nuclear family? **Yes or No**
    - feel anxious or tense if there is too much chaos? **Yes or No**
    - talk with your partner ahead of time about exit strategies if kids fall apart at the 4th long family dinner? **Yes or No**
    - worry about everyone's sleep needs or that your baby will keep everyone in the vicinity up at night with an earache? **Yes or No**

Look at your answers. What do you tend to do?

2. List two ways you unwind or get some QT alone or with family on a group trip.

   _____
   _____

3. Write down two ways you can communicate more clearly with your partner regarding tagging kids, lunch-line logistics, and winding-down time.

   _____
   _____

Time Management Tips

List two things you can you do ahead of time to make packing easier.

_____

What trip categories are appropriate for your packing lists?

_____
_____

Cool Down

1. What is life like in your house the day or two after you return from a vacation?

2. List two strategies that you have for reentry after a vacation that can give you a way to reenter the pace of daily life.

   _____ , _____

APPENDIX A

Fairmeadow United Network 2006–07

It takes a village to raise a child.

The purpose of the Fairmeadow United Network—F.U.N.—is to provide many of the services that used to be provided by a village or extended family in earlier times. F.U.N. makes life a bit easier and more fun through helping hands, sharing the load, and interacting with other parents. Here are the current programs, what they do, and whom to contact to become involved.

Outings

Outings provide moms, dads, couples, or families with an opportunity to get out and do things together. The locations for the groups vary and we are always open to new suggestions.

Family Outings and Get-Togethers   **Frequency:** *twice a season*

Description: A get-together that includes one or more of the following: family board game night; community outreach project; hike at Huddart Park; campout at Fairmeadow School replete with S'mores, campfire songs, and star-gazing

Contacts:

Dad Get-Togethers   **Frequency:** *once a season*

Description: An outing that includes one or more of the following: shoot pool at the Blue Chalk; go to Old Pro and watch a game; play Laserquest with Kids; play Putt Putt Golf with Kids; go to a baseball game at Stanford with Kids

Contacts:

Mom Get-Togethers   **Frequency:** *once a season*

Description: A get-together that includes one or more of the following: lunch or dinner, craft night, and special events such as: Moms v. Kids Softball Game; Creative Memories Scrapbook Workshop; Moms and Kids Beading Night

Contacts:

Playgroups

Playgroups provide children with an opportunity to play together. They are also an excellent time for moms to connect. If you would like to start a new playgroup, provide a contact name and email.

Sibling Playgroups **Frequency/Location:** *Mon. 8:30 a.m.–10:30 a.m. in Mitchell Park*

Description: Weekly sibling playgroup: for younger siblings of Fairmeadow students. Families that will attend Fairmeadow in the future are also welcome. There is interest in starting working parents' playgroup to meet 1x month on weekends. Contact [Name] to set up.

Contacts: Mondays

Weekend:

All-Age Playgroups **Frequency/Location:** *Wed. 1:40 p.m.–3:00 p.m. 2x month at Fairmeadow; Summer Playgroup*

Description: A biweekly playgroup for Fairmeadow students and younger siblings that includes: stomp rockets, bubbles, chalk, beads, face paint, and crafts for all ages. Also dovetails with goodbye parties for Fairmeadow families who move during school year. A weekly Summer Playgroup in Mitchell Park welcomes incoming kindergarten families.

Contacts: Wed. Playgroup:

Summer Playgroup:

Shared Services

Shared services are provided on an as-needed or event-driven basis.

Meals on Wheels **Frequency:** *as needed*
Description: For any family who needs some extra TLC due to illness in family, broken bones, pregnancies, births, or other confidential reasons.
Contacts:

Babysitting Co-Op **Frequency:** *as needed*
Description: A group of families who swap sitting times with fellow Fairmeadow families.
Contacts:

Clothing Exchange **Frequency:** *once in fall*
Description: Gently used clothing exchange at Harvest Fair for Fairmeadow families, including outgrown cleats, roller-blades, ice-skates, etc. Cost $1 per item. Proceeds go to Fairmeadow Family Outreach supplies. Remaining clothes donated to PTA Wardrobe.
Contacts:

Shared Interests

These programs offer a variety of groups and networking contacts. Whether you want to join a group run or just want to find someone to chat with, these contacts can provide you with a group that shares your interest or serve as a starting point.

Informal After-School Sports **Frequency:** *Soccer Wed. after 1:40; Run Club TBD; Basketball TBD*

Kids' Run Prep: meets 1–2x at Cubberly track a few weeks before local kids' running events (i.e., Running of Calves @ Juana Briones).

Soccer: A weekly soccer practice and scrimmage at Fairmeadow for all ages.

Basketball: Weekly basketball practice and scrimmage at Fairmeadow for all ages.

Parent Softball: Co-ed, informal softball; times and location TBD.

Contacts: Kids Run Prep, Soccer, Basketball, Parent Softball

Running Groups/Buddies   **Frequency:** *TBD*   **Description:** Care to find some accountability buddies and train for a short or long race? Or maybe you just want to run for fun. Can set up times privately or join a group run.   **Contacts:** Running Partners:
Walking and Hiking Groups/Buddies   **Frequency/Location:** *TBD*   **Description:** Stretch your legs and network with other moms as we walk to and from the Dish at Stanford. Or go for a hike on the trails with your kids. Join anytime and come whenever you can. No pressure! (Interested in starting a weekly walking group? Contact [Name] to set up).   **Contacts:** (Dish, trails), (hikes in wilderness w/kids), (weekly walking): _____
Book Clubs   **Frequency:** *Book Club: every 8 weeks;*   *Parent Ed Moms Group: every 8 weeks*   **Description:**   1. Book Club—fiction. Rotating leadership. Contact [Name].   2. Parent Ed. Moms' Group with a focus on kids of elementary school age and up. Contact [Name].   **Contacts:** Fiction, Parent Ed

News and Announcements

Whether you want to get the word out about your new baby or announce a meeting, these contacts can help you. See below to find the one that works best for you.

Birth Announcements   **Frequency:** *continuous update*   **Description:** Help Fairmeadow to celebrate the arrival of your new little one with an announcement in the Firebird. Send the names of baby and siblings to Contact's email for the bulletin.   **Contacts:** Firebird Sub-Editor
F.U.N. Bulletin Board   **Frequency:** *continuous update*   **Description:** Use our BB to post upcoming F.U.N. mom, dad, or family events in the Firebird. Please submit details and contact information to Firebird Sub-Editor.   **Contacts:** Firebird Sub-Editor

APPENDIX B

Tantrums

Tantrums and bad moods are a fact of life, but they can drain your energy like nothing else. They are as inevitable as lost socks, and the more strategies you have to deal with them the better. As your children grow, tantrums may disappear only to be replaced by crankiness or moodiness. I call this the Black Cloud syndrome. Strategies that are useful for tantrums can often help with a young person walking around with a black cloud over his head. Here is the list that I've compiled from my own experiences and from many moms in the trenches.

Affirm. Affirm that you are a good mother. You can do this. You are a loving mother. You have a lot of tools. You have the power! Take a deep breath and jump right on in.

Anticipate. If you are mostly rested and on your toes, you can often catch a tantrum early or detect a sibling fight starting. Be ready to divert with humor or distract with a toy, activity, or change of venue or scenery.

Apply a tantrum script. For younger kids, try a script such as, "Use your words. You need to calm down. A tantrum will not get you what you want. You are showing me you're tired and that we may need to leave." For older kids: "Does a tantrum ever get you what you want? Is this worth it? You can choose to stop this tantrum now." I remind my kids that they may finish a tantrum and be done with it, but that there is a COST for me. I feel wiped out and am not going to be up for the fun activities planned for the day. Believe it or not, this works beautifully when they are old enough to begin moving out of tantrums and don't just "see red" (ages three-and-one-half to four).

Assess everyone's energy level and typical daily dip in energy. Maybe your child gets low blood sugar and needs a snack. Maybe one of your children needs more downtime than you or your other kids.

Attention. Do you really have your child's attention? More likely than not, the child is in his or her own gloomy, grumpy world. I ask my child to "look me in the eyes" to make sure that I have his or her attention. I also ask, "Did you hear me, yes or no?" or something to that effect and get the child to repeat what I said. Then I know the child understood the message and is accountable.

Behavior. Be specific about the behavior that is unacceptable. You still love the child unconditionally. "Hitting your sister is unacceptable behavior. She doesn't like it any better than you would." If you can think of a specific instance when the tables were turned, use it.

Boundaries. Set those limits and keep them. You can still provide choices within the established parameters. Kids find comfort in limits and structure, and learning to respect boundaries and recognize limits will help them in the real world. Adapt the boundaries to new ages and stages appropriately.

Charts. Use them. Help your child record how she or he stopped a tantrum or a fight with a sibling and moved on. A week's worth of stickers can mean a trip to get ice cream or the privilege to pick a board game to play or movie to rent. You fill in the blank.

Consequences. Pick immediate consequences. If you put them off to another day or for a whole week, a small child won't understand. Don't say what you don't mean. For example, don't say, "I will never take you to a playground again if you don't stop that tantrum."

Consistency, consistency, consistency. Pick a few household rules (if possible with your partner) and stick with them. Go back to your Philosophy of Parenting (see Chapter 3). This helps you to pick and choose your battles.

Depart if necessary. Be prepared to leave wherever you are if a child cannot turn around his or her noisy, cranky, or unruly behavior. One effective example: "If you can't calm down, then you are showing me you are too tired to stay. Let's calm down by the count of three or we need to go home and rest." Andrea, a mom of two, says, "your behavior is unacceptable," and she makes it time to end the play date or outing. Leave something fun early a few times and your child will remember. You and your other kids may want to stay to see friends, but it really might not be worth it.

> **MOM TIP**
>
> Tell your other children that you all need little sister (or brother) to learn how to behave so that you can take her places together. Since you are now leaving your fun activity early, you can do something special with the other siblings at home while little sister has some quiet time "because she is so tired." This is all about TEAMWORK. If you will be unable to do something with your other children, pull something from your book, toy, or video stash; let them help you make dinner and pick some of the foods; plan an extra play date for them.

Developmental stage. Tantrums do vary in strength and duration. Some children hit a place where they are out of control and cannot hear a word you say. They no longer even know what they are screaming about. As you apply your tantrum script and take deep breaths, remind yourself that this is a developmental stage.

Double D's: Diversion and Distraction. Getting outside, changing the scenery, or taking a car ride with some soothing music can really help if someone is cranky (including you). If you are having trouble getting everyone into a car, make it a galloping or running race. First one buckled in gets to pick the music. First one out of the car gets to unlock the door. Make something funny or fun and kids will perk up before they realize what happened.

Everybody's toys. If you take toys to a playground, remind your child that they are "everybody's toys." If the child wants to take a favorite toy, remind your child ahead of time that he or she can take turns with it or give it to mom, dad, or sitter "if the toy needs a time out."

Favorite toys and what do about them. If child always has trouble sharing a favorite toy, help him or her to put it away before a play date.

Giving in. Don't give in to a tantrum. Your child will remember and prolong a tantrum, trying to get you to do it again.

Humor. For younger kids, turn a childhood favorite song, such as "Twinkle, Twinkle Little Star," into something silly by substituting words such as: "Twinkle, twinkle little toothbrush, how I wonder where your toothpaste is." You can come up with a better one! Older kids appreciate a drier humor. Janet, a stay-at-home mom of three, told her angry, screaming seven-year-old: "Keep screaming that loud. I want to go open the windows so that the neighbors can hear you even better." Her daughter paused and thought about what she was doing. It worked!

Kindness. Model communication in a kind and loving way and your kids will learn important life skills from you. If you do happen to fly off the handle and yell, acknowledge that you are human. Start your day over and begin anew. Apologize if you need to.

Know your child's limits. Too much stimuli, too many people, or too much activity can overwhelm a child and trigger meltdowns.

Mom Story

Linda, a mom of three, has two children who are affected by crowds, noise, and clutter. Before an outing, she gets the lay of the land and assesses whether or not her children will feel comfortable. She also puts a priority on keeping her house picked up and providing downtime. "One of my children is special needs and one has ADHD, so it takes all of my energy to have an organized and calm household. . . . We don't get too busy, and save time for just hanging out (sandbox, Legos™, etc.)."

Name the feeling. If a child is upset, try to get him or her to explain what is causing the upset. Let the child know that you understand it's no fun to feel angry, frustrated, or have your feelings hurt. Little kids, especially, are still learning how to handle the experience of their own emotions. Molly Bang's *When Sophie Gets Angry—Really, Really Angry* . . . or Dr. Seuss's *My Many Colored Days* can help younger kids name their feelings as they talk about the situations in the book. Eric Carle's book *The Grouchy Ladybug*, which has been popular for over twenty years, is a fun way to look at someone who is in a very bad mood and taking it out on others. For older kids, Rachel Simmons' *Odd Girl Speaks Out*, Rosalind Wiseman's *Queen Bees and Wannabees*, Adele Faber and Elaine Mazlish's *How to Talk So Kids Will Listen & Listen So Kids Will Talk*, or William Pollack's *Real Boys: Rescuing Our Sons from the Myths of Boyhood* can help you with some scripts.

Negative behavior. Maybe your kids just need a hug or to be told how much you love them. Watch for negative behavior of your own and replace it with something loving and positive.

Neutral zone. Sometimes your own space gets supercharged. Take your kids to a neutral zone, such as a playground or park, so they can play on shared structures and with "everybody's toys." Everyone can clear his head.

Patterns. Note tantrum patterns and log them down if it helps. Note the time of day, amount of sleep, nap or not, food and drink intake, stimuli, and activity level. Pare down your schedule if you notice that every afternoon after naptime, little S. throws a huge tantrum when leaving the house. Try carpooling with the older ones or just slow everyone's schedule down if you can. The little one may have outgrown tantrums by the next season.

Praise. Praise a child's good behavior and all attempts to improve.

Prepare. Prepare your children for a trip to the store by reviewing your goals. If you are going to get a present for someone, remind your kids that they will only be getting something for someone else. Stick to this plan. Some parents have the "ask once rule." The child may ask once (to do or buy something), but if the parent says, "no," the child is not supposed to ask again. This takes some training, but it does work. You can use the same strategy wherever you are shopping.

Reframe. Sometimes small resentments, crankiness, and tantrums all pile up like bumper cars and everyone is stuck in a mess. Apply the Start Over Strategy. Ask your kids to start the day over, begin anew, wipe the slate clean—and you do it, too. You may need to start your day over several times in one day. Do it anyway. You are trying, and it does pay off.

Role play. Help them to practice reacting to a frustrating situation, such as losing a game, entering a group, handling cliques and bullies. Imagine other uncomfortable social interactions. Try different roles. Let them put on different hats such as cool kid, teacher, or mom and you play your own child, a peer, or a sibling. New ideas that work may bubble up. You can always use topic-related kid and parent books to give you some ideas.

Siblings. If they can't work it out, you can. Separate them. Tell them that all parties involved will lose if they can't resolve whatever it is they are fighting about. Keep an ear open to see if one person might need some extra guidance; sometimes kids really don't have the tools yet to resolve a conflict, and that's where you are key. Get them outside or change the scenery. Have a chat with them about the Golden Rule. Can they think of ways to treat the other more nicely? Is the fight worth irritating your parents?

Time-outs—for you and for your child. When a child has a time-out, she or he is given five or ten minutes to sit quietly and recover. You can do the same thing. Take a deep breath, count to ten, go to another room, call a friend and cry or laugh in the retelling. You can regain your center.

Timer. If kids are having trouble playing with toys together, ask them to take turns using a timer. Taking turns with a timer can be easier to understand than sharing, which is an abstract concept to little kids. Timers are concrete objects, come in lots of shapes, and they're fun and educational. An egg timer where even the littlest can see the time passing is ideal.

Transitions, transitions, transitions. Does your child have trouble with them? Verbal reminders about an upcoming departure time can help. Play the transition out positively. If you are dropping your child off somewhere, a favorite toy or friend can ease the transition. Help your child to buddy up with a childcare worker or another child by planning on staying for a while. You can lessen your helping time at each drop off.

Vending machines and starvation. I wonder how often vending machines trigger meltdowns. Your "starving" kids are looking at all of that enticing food, candy, and soda pop through the clear glass. With younger kids, you can make it a rule to never buy from a vending machine if it is on your usual path. As your kids get older, you can talk about cost and let them use their allowance if they so choose. My children figured out very quickly that all of that hard-earned allowance gets used up quickly with a vending machine purchase or two. Is it worth it? Mine decided "not."

Whining. Children of any age can whine and it can absolutely drive you up the wall. Some moms use the "I can't hear you if you are whining" approach. Others ask the child to "repeat the question using a nice voice." I also use the "you are showing me that you are tired and need fifteen extra minutes of rest time or need to go to bed fifteen minutes early." The latter strategy can also be applied to sibling fights.

Putting all the strategies aside for a moment, I do think that your positive attitude is the key to keeping your emotional state in check when dealing with tantrums and other outbursts. Karen sums it up nicely: "I remind myself that this stage won't last forever."

APPENDIX C

Travel Journals

Travel journals are fun to make and, with a little preparation, easy to keep up with while you are on the road. Kids love them because they can capture their own personal trip experience. You'll see lots of self expression and interest as the journals evolve.

Starting a trip journal. For longer trips, kids can bring a large spiral-bound trip journal in which they can write their observations, draw pictures, or color and glue museum stubs, brochures, local maps, and postcards picked up from various sights. A little prep time beforehand goes a long way. Check out the suggestions below.

FYI: This journal is meant to be banged around and will get well-worn—unlike a Creative Memories Album, which can be an intimidating project that requires more of your supervision. Don't micromanage these: give the kids their materials and let them go with it. Encourage them to use their journal, but don't try to shape it yourself. Give it a shot and help your kids understand what they actually did do and learn this summer.

Download maps from the Internet or make multiple copies out of an atlas. Help kids get oriented—it is ideal to have a global map in the front of the journal for easy reference.

Continental and local maps are great for tracking your travel route. Add a new map for each destination. The kids can draw your travel route on the map and write directions for major turns. Introduce them to the compass rose (the design on a map showing the directions N, S, E, and W) and encourage them to design their own on their maps. They can color maps, too.

Collect things along the way: postcards, brochures, pressed flowers, menus, leaves. This becomes a scavenger hunt for all! At each destination point, find a few postcards of your favorite sites or miniature comical maps of the area. No need to wait for pictures to be developed. These journals work because of their immediacy. If the kids wait until they get home to develop pictures, they are less likely to stay with it.

Get sticky. You can secure pressed flowers, a favorite shell or flat pebble, arrowheads, feathers, or other objects onto pages with clear packaging tape. Tape a booklet about a historical site or local legend into the back of the journal so that the kids can refer to the information in context (and it does not get lost in a bookshelf in the house). Include a local bird-watching guide or seashell identification guide so that kids can keep coming back and learning from the material. Be sure to glue in any artwork created en route: colorings on a restaurant's kid menu, an in situ grave rubbing, pictures of siblings in the car. Expect these journals to be bulky! That is part of their charm.

Helping little kids. If your kids are small, you can write their thoughts in a journal, but make sure you get their own words, when possible. Ask for their reactions to something they saw in a museum or on a hike. Encourage them to draw what they see out the window as you drive.

Older kids can help younger ones with journals and keep their own drawing journal or a scrapbook journal. Older kids can also be in charge of daily expenditures on food and admission fees, and they can track the daily travel budget. Have them include this in their journals.

Brochures have additional materials that kids might not understand until they are older. Include them anyway. This is learning in context. As they go back through journals later on, they will appreciate the knowledge in a different way.

APPENDIX D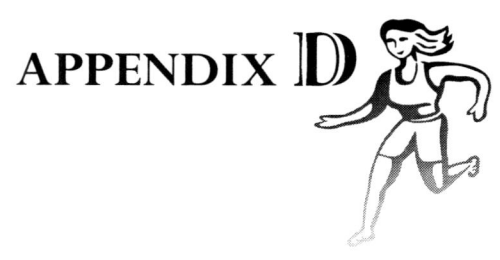

Travel Fun

I always find that you can do a lot with what is at hand, even when traveling. Below I suggest some activities that are great for family gatherings and reunions.

Building

Nothing pleases the imagination like cardboard, tape, and an unpredictable assortment of found items. Use recyclables to build one of these structures:

A town. Use boxes to build a home with many rooms. Cut out windows, doors, and balconies. With tissue paper, create flowers, rivers, and roads. Add string for pulleys and hatches.

A doll house. Make houses out of boxes, then cover with paper bags or construction paper and paint. Make furniture out of cardboard and tape; use clothespins, fabric, and yarn to make dolls. Pillows can be made from cotton balls and mirrors out of aluminum foil.

A space ship. Get a large box or a refrigerator box from a store. Cut windows, add cone, etc., using cardboard and duct tape or packaging tape. Paint with poster paints or spray paint silver. Voila!

A junkyard war. This is a very popular event with older kids. Spend the day making buildings, towers, and armor using recyclables, masking tape, and duct tape. Then stage a battle.

A balloon jungle. Bring along some long, skinny balloons and a few pumps. Blow up the balloons and cover the ceiling, walls, and floor of a room with balloons. Sneak around in it. (Remember, latex balloons are not safe for very young children.)

Games from Scratch

Why stick to published games? You can create your own games while you are on the go. Try some of these ideas:

Card game. Create your own deck of cards, with your own design on back. While you make the deck, brainstorm about new card games.

Board game. Create your own board game, or come up with a variation on a favorite board game. For example, my family has created a version of Monopoly that we called "Kidopoly." Brainstorm the kind of game on paper. You can have numerous discussions while on the road or at the dinner table. You'll want to figure out what makes fun rules, what is the point of the game, what are sound strategies. Write down rules. Make your own cards out of construction paper. Make your game board by cutting up and covering a soda pop bottle or cereal box with construction paper. Design your own game pieces, or use miniature animals or figurines from a toy store. Later, color copy the board and cards and laminate. You can do this at any copy center. Make an extra copy to give to a special friend for the holidays.

Art studio. Combine art and make-believe. Have the kids pretend that they are famous artists. Make collages of cutouts from local magazines, brochures, and unique beverage or food labels. Try to give them a local flavor (for example, use "Nantucket Nectars" if in Nantucket or something to do with lobsters if in Maine). Add some drawing or nature rubbings (can put paper over a tombstone image or leaf and rub a crayon on the paper to create relief image). Create a gallery on the wall and have the artists present their pictures or make them into travel place mats.

A scavenger hunt. Adapt this classic game to your location. Get to know your vacation spot by searching for local items. Great for all ages or older kids can create for younger ones.

Word Play all the Way

Language is a wonderful, portable, recyclable, infinitely variable tool for fun. Make up your own ongoing word games or story lines. When you get an idea, go with it; others will join in and add to it over time. Let a theme develop. No muss, no fuss, and no cleanup afterwards.

In my family, we have a whole mini-language we call **Disney Lingo**. It started with our first trips to Disneyland and just kept growing. It's perfect for Disneyland, of course, but adapts well to just about any trip. It keeps us amused and keeps tired spirits up!

Disney Lingo

Disney Disco — "Are we there yet? How much longer?" refrain, repeated hundreds of times to the tune of "Twinkle, Twinkle Little Star."

Disney Dash — refers to pre-Disney travel hype, or can be applied to the "drop the rope" and rush to the rides time.

Disney Game Plan — Come up with a game plan that includes a list of must-see attractions. Prioritize or rank the list. See what you can see and adapt the game plan as needed. Pace yourselves and include a strategy for an afternoon energy slump. Expect to edit the schedule so that you may still enjoy the course of the day. You will always have something to look forward to when you return to Disney.

Disney Drill — Run through the list: matching tie-dye or neon shirts check; ticket check; safety check; map check; water check; hat, sunglasses, sunscreen check; game plan/strategy check; walkie-talkie or cell phone check; meeting place check; spare food, diaper, clothing check.

Disney Day — One of the longest, high-intensity days of the year where children's nap, meal, or bedtime routines often get tossed. Sometimes Disney Days are consecutive.

Disney Dip — Another name for a dip in energy due to over stimulation, dehydration, long lines, sugar crashes, or minimal sleep the night before the Disney Day.

Disney Bonk — Severe early afternoon Disney Dip, usually for all ages.

Disney Daze — Post-Disney Bonk dazed look.

Disneysaurus/Disneytaurus — What you call one of your small exhausted children who is misbehaving so much that you no longer recognize him/her.

Disney Face Plant — Parent face plants on bed at end of Disney Day.

Disneyitus — Someone with Disneyitus can have one or some of the following symptoms: dehydration, tummy trouble, sore throat, exhaustion, cranky mood.

Disney Checklist — Includes at least 3 Disney Dips or bouts of Disneyitus among group per day.

Disney Delirium — When life is all about acquiring Disney fast passes or beating the crowds on early admission days.

Disney Eyes — When a child grasps a high-priced piece of Disney merchandise that he/she cannot live without and looks at you with those caught-up-in-the-magic Disney Eyes.

Disneymania — A collective body of Disney Delirium, i.e., crowd mentality, particularly evident in crowds of adults donning mouse ears or Goofy hats.

Disneyterrors — When a child becomes attached to a parent because he/she has been terrorized by one of the Disney kid rides.

Disney Aftershock — Disneyterrors that become nightmares post-Disney trip, often involving red beady monster eyes, drawn-out wicked laughs, or pirates with hook hands.

Disneysurvivors — You can find them seated in a back row of an air-conditioned Disney show, or parked under a tree with a cold beverage, ice cream, or frozen lemonade, recharging for the rest of the day.

Disneyglaze — Cotton candy or Churro sugar-coated fingers by people of any age partaking of the full Disney experience.

Disneyburn — adult arms, necks, or backs so sore they "burn," typical of prolonged periods of holding or walking with an oversized, wiped-out, Disney-dazed child.

Disneymagic — When fantasy becomes reality for kids or adults on Disney rides, shows, or at character greetings, also includes the "WOW" factor such as magic carpet rides or flying Tinkerbells; can happen numerous times during the Disney Day and makes the whole experience totally worth it.

Disneyized — A repeat Disney guest who can easily be spotted due to a glazed-eyed happy look despite being in the middle of large sweaty crowds.

Disneyfever — An adult with Disneyfever experiences peak-season Disney trip memory loss, akin to childbirth experiences and subsequent memory loss, and is already planning the next peak-season Disney trip while on the current trip.

Disneyed-out — An adult who is "all done" with Disney's long lines, throngs of people, and lost child escapades.

Disneygrumps — Usually happens on the post-Disney drive with a wiped-out, super-exhausted slew of kids piled in a car. The **Head Grump Award** can actually go to the parent/driver/chauffeur who feels like she/he has been hit over the head with a hammer.

Did You Say Disney?

While we are on the topic of Disneyland, here are some training tips for visiting the magic kingdom during peak season. You know, when everyone is there. These tips are useful when you are visiting any major amusement park for a full day or multiday visit.

Try to begin your trip well-rested and hydrated. You will drain your reserves while at Disney. Upon your return, give yourself a day or two to recharge and get up to speed again. Ease up on your to-do list and plan for some downtime.

While at Disney, take your water breaks. **Disney Days** are hot, lines are long, and excitement is high. It is easy to forget to hydrate. If possible, freeze your water bottles overnight so that they are cold when the heat is scorching.

Train for the afternoon **Disney Bonk**. Utilize your **Disney Game Plan** and have a strategy for the hot afternoon when everyone hits a **Disney Dip**. You can go back to the hotel pool or room for a rest. See an air-conditioned show. Have a leisurely meal. Or escape to California Adventure where the lines are much shorter. Refresh yourself in the Bug's Life water park.

Be a **Disneysurvivor** and plan for some afternoon **Disneyglaze**. The frozen lemonades are particularly refreshing, take a while to eat, and help yourself and the kids to truly cool down. Save your Grizzly River or Splash Mountain fast passes for the heat of the day, when you need to get soaked.

If you hit the **Disneygrumps**, some humor can boost your mood and help you regain perspective. You can have fun developing your own **Disney Lingo**. Check off when someone in your group gets a bit of **Disneyitus**, the **Disney Daze**, or becomes a **Disneytaurus**. It's going to happen. Expect it, try to laugh about it, and move on so that you can continue enjoying the **Disneymagic**.

RESEARCH QUESTIONNAIRE

Finding Energy and Balance in the Weekly Mom Marathon

Name:

Address:

Telephone:

Email:

From whom did you receive this questionnaire?

> I am a 37-year-old mother of four young children ages 1 to 8 years and am collecting information for a writing project that targets mothers of young or school-age children. I want to hear how you mother and juggle the needs of your child(ren), your family, your work, and your ambition/interests.
>
> Thank you in advance for taking the time to answer these questions. If you feel uncomfortable with any, feel free to skip them. Any suggestions regarding this questionnaire or the topic at hand are welcome! I encourage you to pass this form along to other mothers who might be interested in this type of project. This word-of-mouth approach has been working well, and I have already received questionnaires from various parts of the U.S., England, and Australia.
>
> When completed, please email me at gen@sportofmotherhood.com. You are welcome to email me with any questions.

Anonymous Personal Profile Data:

Where a mom is in her mom marathon can make a difference in how she responds to the questions. I feel that my readers would like to know where a particular mom is coming from, and yet I want to protect the identity of the moms who contributed. To accomplish this, one of the appendices will include the profiles of the moms who are quoted/referenced in the book with the names of the people changed, so the profiles are anonymous.

Do you grant permission to publish your profile data anonymously? **Yes or No**

Your current age:

Your age when you had your first child:

Age and gender of your child(ren):

Your work/career pre-children:

Your work/career with children if applicable:

Your work/career hours with children, if applicable: full time or part time, in-home or out-of-home, or a combination of _____?

What has been your status while raising your child(ren): married, single, divorced, widowed, or a combination of _____?

1. Are you a stay-at-home mom, or do you work part time or full time out of the home? If yes to the latter, what kind of work do you do? What are your reasons for working? If you work out of your home, how do you schedule your time to work (i.e., arrange for nanny, sitter, or friend swap; work during nap time, late at night, and/or early in the morning, etc.)?

2. How do you find your energy for the day and for the week? What restores you?

3. As you get older, do you notice a change in your energy level? If so, how do you accommodate that change?

4. How much sleep do you need each night to feel rested? How much do you actually get?

5. How do you pace yourself? Or do you?

6. How do you know when you have "hit the wall" or are at the end of your rope? What do you do about it?

7. How do you pick your commitments?

8. If you were to write your obituary today, can you think of one thing that you would like to have on there that you are not doing today?

9. How have you built your support structure?

10. Do you ever assess your friendships? (Designate accountability buddies, dream buddies, exercise buddies, mentors, cheerleaders, etc.)

11. Do you have any specific tools that help you find balance in your week? (i.e., meet goals, establish priorities, adjust attitude, connect with other moms, prayer, etc.)

12. Do you have any organizational systems (in house and with family) that help you streamline your day?

13. How do you handle resentments? What do they typically involve (conflicting parenting goals/styles, boundaries, responsibilities, societal or familial expectations, etc.)?

14. Do you use affirmations, mantras, and/or prayers to change your attitude or outlook? If so, what are they?

15. Do you have any sources of humor that help you or your family laugh? If so, what are they? (These can be humor websites, comics, comedians, television shows, particular authors, cassettes or CD's, parenting techniques, etc.)

16. What has been the most important thing in helping you be the best mom you can be? It can be anything: a saying, a way of doing things, or a process.

17. Do you have a philosophy of parenting? If so, what is it?

GLOSSARY

24-Hour Strategy. A decision-making tool that buys you some time to think. Before agreeing to a request, politely give yourself 24 hours to think it over.

Accountability Buddy. A person who helps you stay on a specific training program or goal. Her roles may include just showing up, checking on your weekly progress, talking you through roadblocks.

Add Energy/Drain Energy Table. This table helps you to determine how different activities affect your energy. Your goal in working though the table is to discover which activities increase your energy, so that you can move your focus to those positive areas.

Allies. Your allies are your accountability buddies, cheerleaders, and mentors.

Attitude Toolkit. My training kit for giving yourself good attitude skills. It contains five tools: perspective, affirmations, daily readings, humor, and gratitude journals. Using the toolkit gives you an attitude boost.

Cheerleader. A person who encourages and supports your goals. Because she believes in your success, a cheerleader helps you to take risks and to grow.

Compartmentalize. An effective way to separate different aspects of your life from each other and control negative emotions like worry and anger. For example, limit travel worry to travel days.

Dream Team. A term I use to describe a really focused, on-board support team. Tighter than a support network.

EFFECT. This is a checklist to help you assess the workability of any possible new commitments. See Chapter 5.

Flexibility Threshold. The point at which someone stops adapting well to things around them. It's especially important to know when traveling with a group. See Chapter 9.

Fool Factor. The dampening effect of worrying about what others think. Reduces your ability to take good risks or put yourself out there. It's usually an indication that you are outside your comfort zone and taking new steps in a good direction. Fight the Fool Factor.

Friendship Assessment. A simple table designed to help you understand the characteristics of your friendships. The assessment gives you a better sense of the roles different friends can play in your support network—a good exercise in clear thinking about relationships.

Goal Calendar. This can be a wall calendar, desk calendar, date book, or computer-generated calendar. It becomes your place for recording the time you set aside for your training and goals: a key tool to see what you've accomplished and to plan future training. Time recorded is all-inclusive: training, thinking, researching, reassessing, and goal celebration time all go on your calendar.

Hitting the Wall. In a foot race, hitting the wall means suddenly running out of energy and strength. In marathons, mile 18 is known as "The Wall" because it is where many runners feel completely exhausted. Moms too hit the wall, and can train for it. Walls that moms face are much more complicated than mile 18, but I divide them into three categories: situational walls, such as a bout of the chickenpox, a car breaking down, a computer crash, or a family gathering; seasonal walls, such as the beginning or end of school-year rush, tax time, or holiday madness; and life-changing walls, such as a chronic diagnosis, death, or divorce.

Laughing Library. Funny family stories that the kids collect and retell. These stories are great morale boosters and can start a story-telling tradition in your family.

Mentor. A person who guides, inspires and educates you in one of your goal categories or interests.

Minimum/Bonus Strategy. This *Sport of Motherhood* strategy helps you set a reasonable pace and stay on track to success. Pick a realistic weekly minimum goal time so that you can maintain your progress week after week. Additional goal time is bonus. You can apply the Minimum/Bonus Strategy to any goal. Whether you meet your weekly minimum or go beyond it into bonus time, you are successful.

Mission Statement. I recommend that formal support groups compose a mission statement to define the group's purpose and unify its members. The mission statement can be written in the first couple of meetings.

Personal Time. Your downtime. You need time to put your feet up to think, to rest, to create. Get a little bored and see what bubbles up. Create white space on your calendar and protect that personal time.

Philosophy of Parenting. The structure of values and priorities that you apply both to your overall family life and to the daily business of child-rearing. Without a philosophy of parenting, your parenting decisions can be inconsistent.

Power-Goaling. This occurs when one activity serves several personal goals. An example would be going for a walk with a friend in the woods. This single activity could serve three goals for someone: getting exercise, connecting with friends, and enjoying nature.

Pressure Points. Pressure points are recurring problems or obstacles. You can deal with them in your training plan.

Priority Rankings. The ranking of your goals in order of their importance to you.

Progress. Progress is a journey, therefore any time spent working towards a goal is progress. *The Sport of Motherhood* defines progress as the process, not the result. Encouragement + Accountability = Progress.

Red Flags. These are situations that consistently push you to hit the wall. You can train yourself to recognize them.

Reentry. Your plan for returning home and resuming everyday life after travel.

Seasons of Motherhood. The idea that mothers are living through different seasons in their lives and the lives of their children. Helps busy moms to gain perspective and select which goals to pursue now and which to defer to a more fitting season in their family's development.

Sleep Ideal. This is the amount of sleep that you need each night. You can find your sleep ideal by finding an opportunity to sleep naturally (without an alarm clock) for four or five days, record how long you sleep each night, and then calculate your average hours of sleep per night.

SPICE List. The SPICE List groups the essential foods in the Whole Mom Food Groups. These foods nourish all aspect of mothers, together making our whole person healthy and strong. The SPICE List is a key tool in helping you set up a personal Strategic Plan. The items on the SPICE List are: Spiritual Nurturance, Physical Nutrition and Exercise, Intellectual Stimulation, Communal Sustenance, and Emotional Comfort.

Start-Your-Day-Over Strategy. Stop a downhill trend with this strategy. The basic tactics are: stop, take a few breaths, shake off the bad emotions, and start the day over. Can be done multiple times a day, and works for the whole family.

Strategic Plan. Your strategic plan is a roadmap to your goals. It lays out where you want to go, the steps you'll take to get there, the potential obstacles you'll meet and how you will overcome them. It articulates both what you want to accomplish and how you can do it. It's your training plan.

Strategic Plan Table. A matrix that helps you to organize your strategic plan by breaking it down into stages and assessing resources. Extremely useful for comparing goals, finding redundant resources, and setting priorities. Categories in the table are your **Goal**, **Getting There**, **Status**, **Obstacles**, **Resources**, **Allies**, **Next Step**, and **Pay Off**.

Time-Use Grid. A weekly schedule that helps you make the time you need to start on your new goals.

Travel Readiness Assessment. A set of questions to help you decide what kind of family travel you and your family are ready for. A tool for vacation planning.

Triple Hitter Strategy. Try things three times before giving up on them—a good strategy when you are joining a new group or starting a new activity.

Whole Mom Food Groups. This is the balanced diet we need to be whole and healthy moms. These five food groups feed all the different aspects of ourselves. Just as our physical bodies need a balanced diet of proteins, fruits, vegetables, and grains, we need nourishment from these "food" groups to be healthy. They spell SPICE:

- **S**piritual Nurturance
- **P**hysical Nutrition and Exercise
- **I**ntellectual Stimulation
- **C**ommunal Sustenance
- **E**motional Comfort